10 to 4

Brett Favre's Journey from Rotten Bayou to the Top of the NFL

By Mark McHale

With Brett Favre and Tim Stephens

Indigo Publishing Group, LLC

Publisher	Henry S. Beers
Associate Publisher	Richard J. Hutto
Associate Publisher	Rick L. Nolte
Executive Vice President	Robert G. Aldrich
Operations Manager	Gary G. Pulliam
Editor-in-Chief	Joni Woolf
Designer	Audra George
Marketing & Media	Mary Robinson

Library of Congress Control Number: 2007938386

ISBN: (13 digit) 978-1-934144-24-4
       (10 digit) 1-934144-24-X

Indigo Publishing Group books are available at quantity discounts with bulk purchase for educational, business, or sales promotional use. For information, please write to: Indigo Publishing Group, LLC, 435 Second Street,
Suite 320, Macon, GA 31201, or call 866-311-9578.

Cover photograph by: David Stluka
Cover design by: Audra George
Back cover illustration by: Eli Cloud (www.blurstorm.com)

For Beverly, my wife, who patiently waited for the book to be written, and to all the unknown football stars who just wanted a chance. A special thanks to Brett's high school coach and father, Irvin Favre, and to my high school coach, Walter Barr. Both coaches have been great inspirations to me and my football career.

Table of Contents

Acknowledgments

I would like to thank the following individuals for their tireless work in making this book a reality:

Brett Favre for believing in himself enough to do what it took to become the great player he is and for sitting down with me for countless interviews.

The Favre family for their treasured friendship through the years.

Jim Carmody, Keith Daniels and the rest of the men I coached with at the University of Southern Mississippi.

Lauren Lipton for transcribing hours of interview sessions with Brett Favre and others.

Tim Stephens for his writing expertise, prayers, support and friendship.

Lauren Lipton

Dave Wellman for his efforts editing this book.

Rick Nolte for his guidance in getting this story published.

Les Steckel, whose book "One Yard Short", provided an outline for this book.

The Fellowship of Christian Athletes for their service to God and influence on me.

— Coach Mark McHale

Foreword

All I ever wanted was a chance and Coach Mark McHale gave it to me. For that, I am grateful. Had Coach McHale not wandered by an out-of-the-way high school football field in Kiln, Mississippi, I probably never would have had a career in the NFL.

My story is one of perseverance. Not just mine, but Coach McHale's. He could have quit recruiting me at any time and no one would have blamed him. I was the final player offered a scholarship by the University of Southern Mississippi and then only when another player declined USM's offer. No one would have missed me. But Coach McHale didn't quit.

When other coaches told him I couldn't play at the NCAA Division I-A level, Coach McHale still believed in me and fought for me. When I was one of more than one dozen quarterbacks being recruited, Coach McHale kept talking me up. When Southern Miss had a limited number of campus visits scheduled for recruits, Coach McHale made sure I received one of them.

Coach McHale's faith in me, even against the longest of odds, was astounding. But that's the kind of coach, the kind of man, Mark McHale is. He is a man of faith. He is a man of perseverance. He is a man who believes in something greater than himself.

(Al Bello/Getty Images)

Brett Favre reached the pinnacle of the NFL when he led the Green Bay Packers to victory against the New England Patriots in Super Bowl XXXI.

When I think back to those days at my high school football field, it's almost as if that was someone else. Sure, I had the drive to succeed, I had the desire to play at the next level, but it took more than me wishing and hoping that would happen. Someone had to take notice. If I labored in obscurity, I wouldn't have received a scholarship. All I needed was one person, one coach, one recruiter to take notice. Just one.

That one was Coach McHale.

Why he stuck with me, I'm not sure. During the first game he saw me, I didn't throw a half-dozen passes the entire night. Now, I throw more than that in a single drive. Yet Coach McHale kept coming back. He saw something in me that he liked. Who knows how many players he passed up to keep coming to see me? I'm certainly glad he did.

My career – my life – has taken some wild turns. I almost didn't get a scholarship, but that was nothing compared to being near death, struggling in a hospital bed while my teammates prepared to play. Had it not been for my brother, Scott, pulling me from a mangled car, I probably wouldn't be here. Had it not been for my dad, Irvin, pushing me to be better, I likely wouldn't have made it to college, let alone the NFL. Had it not been for my mom, Bonita, teaching me right from wrong, I might be in jail. Had it not been for Coach McHale sticking with me I might never have played football after high school.

From Rotten Bayou to the Super Bowl. That just doesn't happen. At least it's not supposed to happen. But it did and there are so many people to thank. There are so many people who helped me get to the point where I am today. The memories flood back and overwhelm me. I've been fortunate. I've been blessed. My career has been a tremendous journey of one surprise after another. Sometimes all I can do is shake my head and laugh about it all.

All I ever wanted was a chance. One chance. One opportunity. One moment to show what I could do. Those opportunties don't come along often in life. When they do, you have to be ready. You have to be prepared.

And you have to persevere. That's what I did. That's what Coach McHale did.

That Coach McHale has put this story in book form is amazingly gratifying. If it inspires another youngster to strive to fulfill a dream, then it will be a success. It can't be anything but a success.

— *Brett Favre*

Introduction

In the field of professional sports, there are numerous stories of athletes reaching the height of stardom. Most were heavily recruited record breakers in high school with their pick of a university.

This story is different. Astonishingly different. This is a story of a quarterback who not only wasn't highly recruited but who had merely one major college scholarship offer, an offer that set in motion an amazing series of events that began on the field of a rural Mississippi high school and that will culminate with his induction into the Pro Football Hall of Fame.

This is the story of Brett Favre.

Brett, a Super Bowl-winning quarterback, three-time NFL Most Valuable Player and eight-time Pro Bowl selection, was the last recruit taken in the University of Southern Mississippi's 1987 recruiting class. Had a linebacker from Atlanta accepted our offer, Brett might never have signed to play major college football. As it was, he didn't receive a scholarship offer until the eve of National Signing Day.

Brett jumped at the chance to play just 70 miles from his home at his parents' alma mater. He began his college career as the seventh-string quarterback. Most players in that situation either quit or move to another position and Southern Miss coaches had Brett ticketed to play linebacker. Brett, though, impressed early at quarterback, then beat overwhelming odds to rapidly climb the depth chart and start in just the third game of his freshman season.

We'll never know where Brett would have ended up had he not received a scholarship to Southern Miss. Had just one event in his incredible story been changed, the world likely never would have heard of the Green Bay Packers' star of Super Bowl XXXI.

How do I know all this? I'm the coach who was blessed to have recruited Brett to Southern Miss. What began as a relationship between a coach and a player has grown into a true, deep friendship with Brett and his family. I'm honored to be a part of it and am privileged to share it with you.

— *Coach Mark McHale*.

Chapter 1

Super Bowl XXXI

My ears were irritated by the constant humming of the airplane engine. The noise level increased and decreased just enough to make hearing any conversation difficult. I hated flying in these small planes. Being crammed into a seat with no room to cross my legs and no way to get comfortable no matter how much I squirmed was no way to travel.

My thoughts shifted from my discomfort to the voices shouting across the aisle. Twenty-some passengers were trying to talk at the same time and while I don't usually eavesdrop, I was interested in what this group had to say. All of my fellow passengers on this flight from Atlanta were clad the same way – in the green and gold of the Green Bay Packers. Two wore jerseys featuring the No. 4. Others wore hats, jackets, sweatshirts and other items sporting the familiar Green Bay oval "G."

I leaned toward the aisle, trying to pick up any bits of conversation I could. My interest came not only from being a football coach, but as the one who had recruited Packers' quarterback Brett Favre to the University of Southern Mississippi. Those No. 4 jerseys were replicas of Brett's jersey. Just as I would get interested

Coach Mark McHale

in a conversation, it would be smothered by what I call one of life's "hemos," short for hemorrhoid. In other words, a pain in the butt. Life contains many hemos and this was one of them.

I would have assumed that the group was headed to Super Bowl XXXI, where Brett and the Packers were set to play the New England

Patriots. That would have been a reasonable assumption had the plane been bound for New Orleans. We, though, were destined for Hattiesburg, Miss. Finally, I had to ask the couple sitting in front of me if they were headed to the Super Bowl. Their response was an enthusiastic, "we sure are and we're excited!" I asked why, then, were they flying to Hattiesburg, 110 miles north of New Orleans?

"All the fans on this plane are going to visit Southern Miss to see where Brett played college ball," the husband said. "We're going to drive from there to Kiln, Mississippi to see his home. We plan on getting some sod or dirt from there as souvenirs."

I couldn't believe what I was hearing! I didn't tell them I was the coach who had recruited Brett. With the noise level what it was, I didn't want to have to yell everything over the hum of the engines, so I just kept that to myself and marveled at what I was experiencing.

 **Fact 4 Favre**

One day after his father Irvin died of a heart attack, Brett Favre passed for 399 yards and four touchdowns in a 41-7 victory against the Oakland Raiders in a Monday night game on Dec. 22, 2003.

I looked out the window and the flat terrain and the pine trees approached as we descended toward the Pine Belt Airport. My day had started in Kentucky where I had just accepted a job as an assistant coach at the University of Louisville. Leaving Southern Miss after my second coaching stint there was difficult, but Louisville presented a great opportunity.

Between my first stop at Southern Miss in 1986 and my return there in 1996, I had coached in the World Football League, at the University of South Carolina, the Canadian Football League and back in the WFL. I recruited Brett in 1987 and left five years later for the Montreal Machine of the WFL. Montreal's offensive coordinator was Joe Clark, who had been an assistant coach for Lindy Infante, head coach of the Packers. I also had coached with Joe when we were with the Frankfurt Galaxy and Amsterdam Admirals, and we often talked about his days with Green Bay.

For a while, the CFL placed some franchises in the United States. I coached with the Shreveport Pirates and the head coach was Forrest Gregg, the Hall of Fame offensive tackle with the Packers under legendary Coach Vince Lombardi. Coach Lombardi called Forrest "by far the best football player I ever coached." Forrest was selected

(Andy Hayt/Getty Images)

Brett Favre leaps into the arms of a teammate to celebrate a touchdown run that proved to be the winning points for Green Bay in its victory against New England in Super Bowl XXXI.

All-Pro nine times, making him the only Packer named All-Pro more than Brett. Being an offensive line coach, I was fascinated that Coach Lombardi would make such a statement since he coached skilled players such as Paul Hornung and Bart Starr. I constantly asked Forrest about what kind of man Coach Lombardi was. Later, when I coached at Louisville, I met Hornung and exercised beside him at U of L from time to time. I peppered him with questions about the Packers and his playing days.

Picking the brains of people of that caliber was fun. Ernie Stautner, our head coach when I was with Frankfort, is another Hall of Famer who received the same inquisitive treatment. Packer fans know that Coach Lombardi and Tom Landry, another Hall of Famer as coach with the Dallas Cowboys, were on the same staff with the New York Giants. Coach Stautner was Coach Landry's defensive coordinator with Dallas and I loved talking with him about his playing and coaching days. He often talked of the rivalry between coach Landry and coach Lombardi.

The plane's tires squealed as they touched the hot surface of the landing strip. I took a quick glance at my watch and it was 10 to 4. We landed right on time. I couldn't wait to get home. The last six months had been strenuous. Recruiting season kicked into high gear just as football season ended. Also, I had changed jobs right in the middle of recruiting season. People ask what a coach does in the offseason. I tell them it is every bit as intense as the regular season because recruiting leaves little time to relax. This week, I had until Monday to catch up on some relaxation.

The plane turned at the end of the runway and headed toward the terminal. I could see my wife Beverly inside. She was experiencing some tough times, too. She grew up in Eatonville, Miss., just four miles from this airport. We married while I was at South Carolina and I moved her from her hometown to Columbia, S.C., to Shreveport, La., before getting her back home when I returned to Southern Miss. We built a nice house on a lake in a golf course community in Hattiesburg. Beverly worked with the contractors while I coached two-a-day practices. We moved into the house in September and four months later I took the job at Louisville. Not many coaches get to essentially live in their wife's hometown. That house was Beverly's baby. She had done everything from picking out the brick, flooring, light fixtures, colors and landscaping. I knew that moving was killing her but she never complained. She is so supportive and understanding of the coaching profession. It takes a special person to be married to a coach and she is special.

I was excited to get a hug from this petite, blue-eyed blonde beauty from the South. We got my luggage and headed for our temporary home. I told her about the fans on the plane and she told me that while I was in Louisville all week Green Bay fans had flooded the Southern Miss campus. They bought every souvenir they could find.

"I've never seen anything like it," Beverly said.

Beverly drove me to USM's stadium where I was scheduled to speak at a press conference at the Letterman's Club Building about the recruitment of Brett. I couldn't believe the throng of reporters. Cameras and microphones were everywhere. The interview lasted about 15 minutes. I was eager to get out of there and get home. It had been a long day. As we pulled up to the house, I thought of how important it was to get our home sold. I quickly put those thoughts aside and got a good night's sleep, anticipating the Super Bowl the next day.

Beverly and I went to church the next morning, Jan. 26, then to her family's home for lunch. All the talk was about Brett and the Super Bowl. Even Beverly's family didn't know the details of my recruitment of Brett. Very few people did. After some quality time with family, we headed home to watch the Super Bowl. At 10 to 4 I sat down to watch the pre-game show. I had asked Beverly not to let anyone disturb me until the game was over. This game was of special importance because Brett was in it.

There I sat, kicked back in my recliner with all the snacks and drinks I needed to watch the Super Bowl. Then the phone rang. Beverly came in to tell me somebody was seriously interested in buying our house and wanted to come look at it. We didn't even have a "for sale" sign in the yard. How did they even know it was for sale? I took the phone and the man on the other end said he read in the newspaper that I was going to Louisville and that he lived in the same neighborhood. He sounded serious about buying and I knew we had to sell, the quicker the better. I was returning to Louisville on Monday and it would be incredibly sweet to sell the house so quickly.

I told him to come over. He did and explained that he had to sell his house because of personal reasons but he loved the neighborhood and wanted to stay in it. I asked if he wanted a tour and he said he didn't need to look because our home was so similar to his. That struck me as strange, but I told him the asking price and he said, "I'll take it." I'd been through the house-selling process many times and it just never happened like this. We shook hands and I promised to have the papers drawn up on Monday. That was that. What a blessing!

I hurried back to my recliner.

"I don't care what else comes up, I'm not going to stop watching until the game is over," I told Beverly.

Much of the pre-game show focused on Brett and Patriots' quarterback Drew Bledsoe. The more they talked about Brett, the more I reminisced about the amazing story of him going from Hancock North Central High School to Southern Miss, then to the NFL. Not many knew the whole story of how Brett went from a small-school player who wasn't recruited to a scholarship quarterback at Southern Miss. I began to daydream about it. It was like watching a movie.

> **"The blessings come upon me and overtake me."**
> **– Deuteronomy 28:2.**

BRETT'S VIEW

I look at my career and the way it started out and it's hard to believe it's turned out the way that it has. I wasn't recruited by a bunch of schools. I was barely recruited by Southern Miss.

I remember getting to Southern Miss and looking around and

thinking, "man, this doesn't look too good." No one much knew who I was and the coaches hadn't exactly been beating down my door. I was aware of those things, but I knew, too, that you don't have to throw for 4,000 yards to make it, either.

It's funny how it worked out. If I had had 10 different schools offer me scholarships and I had picked Alabama or something like that I might never have seen the field. It happens to guys every year. They go to these big schools where it's hard to play period. Then the stars have to line up just right for a guy to get a chance to get on the field.

On the other hand, maybe the guy in the next county throws for more yards and more touchdowns and you don't get recruited at all. You don't sign a scholarship. Maybe you go to a small junior college. If it's meant to be, it's meant to be. The only thing you can control is what you need to do. You can't point fingers and things like that. It's just the way it is.

I kind of knew what I was up against and I told myself that if I ever

(Photo by Beverly McHale)

Brett Favre has been the subject of dozens of magazine covers during his NFL career with the Green Bay Packers. Many of these are displayed in his home as well as those of family members.

got the chance I'd make the most of it. That's all you can do. You can't make them play you. You can't make them recruit you.

I knew all that and at times it didn't look good for me, but look what happened. The Super Bowls. The Pro Bowls. You see people walking around wearing a No. 4 jersey with my name on it. It's pretty amazing. I can't get used to it all. I can't say I ever get used to all the attention. I wonder, "Why me? Why me, a kid from Kiln, Mississippi? Why me, a kid who threw for 300 yards playing in a wing-T and wishbone offense?"

I guess part of it was determination. I was determined to get to this point if someone would just give me a chance. Just give me that

(Photo by Beverly McHale)

Brett Favre and the Green Bay Packers were honored with the cover of a Wheaties box following their Super Bowl XXXI triumph.

chance. I was up against a lot of people and a lot of things sometimes, but never once did I say I couldn't do it. Never once. A lot of times I probably should have felt that way, but I was determined that if I ever got that chance, I was going to make the most of it.

It's amazing. No one knew who I was. No one but Coach McHale really recruited me. Now, people come up and want pictures and autographs and things like that. It's an odd feeling for me. I'm not one to be rude to people. I don't try to be disrespectful or anything like that. It's not my nature to be that way.

At one time nobody knew who I was, now it's hard to go to a movie or out to eat. Deanna and I aren't complete recluses, but sometimes we kind of have to be. I'm fine with it. It's part of the territory. It's more than I ever asked for, but I can't complain about it. I still try to treat people the right way.

I always had confidence I could play pro ball. There's no doubt that that confidence comes from Mom and Dad. I sort of compare it to my cousin David. He could fix a radio when he was 12 years old. His dad was an electrician, did construction work, stuff like that. If it was broken, David could fix it. As I got older, it kind of dawned on me that you kind of apply a trade by being influenced by your surroundings from day one. Early on, I knew how to wear a baseball glove. I knew how to break it in. I knew how to dress as a baseball player. I knew you didn't wear your pants a certain way. I knew what went with what. I knew how to wear a baseball cap, the proper technique to bunt, how to throw a football. I didn't know how to read defenses, but I knew how to be tough and I knew what it would take. I didn't necessarily know how to be a leader at the time. It just kind of came natural.

I never missed a day of school. Not that I really liked school, I just didn't want to miss something. I didn't want to miss practice and give someone else a chance to take my position. I wanted to be the guy.

Dad coached baseball in the summer and we were always around the right way to do things. Because of that, I never liked to lose. I remember being little and being the ball boy or bat boy for Dad's teams and when we'd lose I'd take it harder than they did. Dad might not have known it, but I went back in my room and cried because we lost the state American Legion championship when I was 5 years old. I hated to lose and that just got greater the older I got.

Also as I got older, I became aware that I could only control what I do. That's disappointing to me even to this day. I could control how I throw the ball, make a tackle or a block, whatever. I could control that, but I wanted to be in control of our defense stopping the opposing offense and I couldn't do that. That was disappointing to me because of my competitive nature and I wouldn't change it, but it's been stressful. It must be like being a head coach. You're trying to manage all this stuff and it's hard to do. As a coach, you're teaching a guy to block and he's missing his block because of poor technique so you just want to go out and do it for him, but you can't.

As for the Super Bowl, it was played in New Orleans and that's as close to home as I can get. That went through my mind all the time that season. From the start of the season I knew we had a good shot anyway, but that the Super Bowl was going to be in New Orleans, for us to get there would be too good to be true. I've said that about my whole career. From the Tulane game as a USM freshman up until now it's been just about perfect. It's just been meant to be so I keep plugging along. I hardly ever stopped and questioned it because it is what it is. I quit questioning it a long time ago. I do what I can and try to give myself the best chance I can to succeed. It all amazes me.

Chapter **2**

Reminiscing

I hearkened back to my time at Appalachian State University in Boone, N.C., where I was offensive coordinator and offensive line coach. It was 1986. I had just accepted a job at East Carolina University and until I sold my house in Boone and bought another, I lived in the Ramada Inn in Greenville, N.C. Our off-season program ended in February, followed by spring practice in March and April. May meant hitting the road to recruit.

May is when coaches venture out of their designated recruiting areas to filter out players who'll be seniors in the fall. The process takes place all over the country. While this May I was recruiting for East Carolina, someone else was doing the same thing for Southern Miss.

After May recruiting I went to Myrtle Beach, S.C., with my best friend, Bugs Moffett for a week of sun and fun. When I got back to Greenville, I learned a contract I had on a house I wanted to purchase had fallen through. I didn't realize it at the time, but it was a blessing in disguise. I had only been back a couple of hours when I received a call from Keith Daniels, the offensive coordinator at Southern Miss. USM's offensive line coach had just left for Clemson and someone had recommended me as a replacement.

I had been at East Carolina just more than four months and I wasn't very familiar with Southern Miss. I knew there was a Mississippi, Mississippi State and a Southern Miss, but I didn't have any idea which one was where. I had coached all my life in West Virginia, Virginia and North Carolina. I'd never been to Mississippi. I told Keith I'd think about it.

Bugs asked what the call was about. Bugs was in the beer business and is a good ol' soul, but like a lot of people, knew little about the coaching business. He asked, "the university of who?" At that point, I didn't know much more than Bugs, but I knew East Carolina played Southern Miss, so I headed to the ECU football office to look at a media guide. I read that Southern Miss was in Hattiesburg, about 60

(Courtesy of www.markmchalefootball.com)

Recognized among the top offensive line coaches in the country, McHale has coached in eight bowl games for such schools as Southern Mississippi, South Carolina, Marshall and Florida State.

miles from the Gulf Coast, and through the years had played Florida State, Auburn, Georgia, Florida, Texas A&M, Alabama and other premier programs. I also learned that Southern Miss had experienced just five losing seasons in its history. I couldn't believe it. Few programs could boast such a record.

Bugs told me if I took the job our next vacation would have to be in New Orleans, which was fine with me, as that was another factor in Southern Miss' favor. I was intrigued about coaching in the South, but East Carolina's football coach was Art Baker, one of the finest gentlemen I'd ever known. I had tremendous respect for him and wondered how I would tell him I was interviewing for another job after just four months.

The more I read on Southern Miss, the more interested I became. I called Keith and told him I would interview, then called Coach Baker, who tried to talk me out of going before telling me to check out the opportunity. After six years in the North Carolina mountains at Appalachian State, my body had adjusted to the cold. ECU was a bit warmer, but when I got off the plane in Mississippi it was body shock. There was no airflow and the sun penetrated me. Wide receivers coach Jack White picked me up at the airport in Jackson, Miss., and drove me to Hattiesburg. I surveyed the landscape, which was all flat land and pine trees, a stark contrast to the mountains to which I was accustomed. Jack had the air conditioning on full blast and I still was sweating. I was starting to wonder if I really wanted this job.

Jack told me Southern Miss ran an option offense, with not much of a passing attack other than a little play action and sprint outs. My background was in pro-style, dropback passing offenses. I met Head Coach Jim Carmody and his staff, then watched some tapes from the previous season with Keith. I tried to concentrate on the offensive line, but the quarterback, Reggie Collier, jumped out at me as one of the greatest athletes I'd ever seen. He did things that were unbelievable, even against Alabama. He had a strong arm, too. I asked about him and Keith told me Reggie was a senior and would not be back next season. Several quarterbacks were returning, but none comparable to Reggie.

I returned to Greenville and weighed my decision. Southern Miss was coming off a 7-4 season and had a lot of players back. I wanted to coach in the South. I wanted to coach against the kinds of teams Southern Miss played. Keith called to offer me the job and I jumped at the opportunity.

> **"... We do not know what to do, but we look to You."**
> **– 2 Chronicles 20:12.**

BRETT'S VIEW

Reggie Collier.

When I was thinking about going to college, Reggie Collier was fresh on my mind. You know, a lot of the kids today don't even remember him, but he was maybe one of the best college football players ever, so there was appeal to Southern Miss for me because of him.

I would have loved to have gone to Southern Miss. Mom and Dad went there, so I probably was a little more partial to it. There were the big three schools in the state – Ole Miss, Mississippi State and Southern Miss. I liked Southern Miss but I'd have gone anywhere. Southern Miss was close to home, Mom and Dad had gone there. Reggie Collier had played there.

I remember Coach McHale coming down a number of times. I don't remember everything that was said, but I know he was the only coach coming by to see me. I didn't want to do anything that made him say, "Aw, this guy is terrible," or something like that. I was happy that Coach McHale was looking at me. For me, Southern Miss was big-time

The sign for Favre's on the Bayou is the lone remnant of the restaurant the family owned near their Mississippi home. The establishment was a casualty of Hurricane Katrina in 2005. Brett Favre helped recovery of the area by staging numerous benefits that raised hundreds of thousands of dollars.

football. Maybe they weren't Notre Dame or Florida State or Miami or USC, but it was plenty good enough for me. There weren't too many coaches knocking on my door. If Coach McHale hadn't come when he did, I don't know what would have happened. I was eager to play and some other schools had sent me letters and stuff, but no one really came by. I was just happy Coach McHale was there.

We lived out in the country on 55 acres in a house built in 1948. We lived on a bayou that led into the river that flowed into the Bay of St. Louis. There were alligators and snakes. It was a way of life.

When I came home after Hurricane Katrina (in 2005), it was terrible. I didn't recognize the area any more. The landscape had changed. The houses were gone. The streets had washed away. Bridges were gone. In our house, we had eight feet of water. There were dead snakes and fish in the house. It's really hard to believe that could happen, how it could all change like that.

I had to do something. I've been fortunate. We sent I don't know how many 18-wheelers loaded with stuff down there. We helped some schools a lot.

Chapter **3**

Recruiting

When I arrived back in Hattiesburg, I met with Thamas Coleman, our linebackers coach, to get familiar with my recruiting duties. Recruiting is the bloodline of all college football programs and requires diligence and organization. It is the hardest thing to adjust to in a new job.

College football is sponsored by 806 schools and 75 percent are at the NCAA Division II level or lower. It is rare for an athlete capable of playing college ball not to be evaluated by a recruiter, usually several recruiters. While a coach might misjudge a player's talent level, rarely does a prospect go unnoticed. My job was to find recruits who not only could play for Southern Miss, but who could compete against the major programs on our schedule.

 **Fact 4 Favre**

Brett Favre played five years of varsity baseball in high school, starting and leading the team in hitting. He was a three-year, two-way starter in football.

Each coach has a geographical area he recruits. Thamas handed me my list, for which I was responsible for keeping updated, a challenge being that coaches often change jobs, schools consolidate, close, etc. It takes a while to get to know an area and I already had a lot of catching up to do. My area included all Mississippi schools from Hattiesburg to the Gulf Coast, as well as New Orleans, which had 75 schools by itself. I also had the bayou south of New Orleans and all schools to the west below I-10 to Baton Rouge. That's a lot of schools and many weren't easy to get to. I also discovered I needed to learn a new language when I headed deep into Cajun country, as names are pronounced much differently in Louisiana than they are in the Virginias and Carolinas.

Thamas also gave me a list of prospects from a national scouting service. This list is compiled by mailing cards to all high school head coaches and asking them to list upcoming seniors they felt could play college ball. There was room for the player's name, height, weight, 40-yard dash time, grade point average and ACT or SAT score. Coaches

Athletics were never far from the center of the Favre family for Irvin, Bonita and the kids. Scott and Brett are standing behind their parents while Jeff and Brandi are on Mom's lap.

(Favre family photo)

also were asked to rank at what level they thought the players might be able to play.

Sorting through the list was a challenge because the schools were listed alphabetically by state and the names and phone numbers weren't always accurate. Still, the list was helpful. I had a lot of phone calls to make.

Thamas also handed me a stack of questionnaires from any player who had expressed an interest in Southern Miss. Questionnaires are valuable tools in that they offer a wealth of information on the players, including their academic standing, a factor that eliminates a number of players right away. The players fill out the top five schools in which they're interested, list the position they'd like to play, etc. One of the questions asks what the player's major would be. I've seen prospects list "engineering" and when asked what kind, they said they'd like to drive a train.

Thamas also gave me two boxes of video tapes collected by the coach I replaced, Bill D'Andrea. He had collected them while recruiting during the spring. I watched them to help evaluate the players I wanted to recruit. A coach must know who is a solid prospect, a possible prospect and a non-prospect in order to manage how much time will be spent where. For a sure-fire prospect, a coach visits the guidance counselor and goes by a practice or a game. For a prospect on the bubble, a recruiter will go to a practice or game but likely spend less time than he would with a player he definitely wants to sign. If a school has no players a coach is interested in, the coach still will visit the school for the public relations value but won't spend a great deal of time there. Organization and efficiency are at a premium and I had a lot of catching up to do.

Next, I had to crosscheck the list of players committed to attending our football camp and see who was from my area, if they were a scholarship candidate or on the bubble. Then I worked from D'Andrea's master list of prospects in whom we were interested. The list contained about 75 names from my area. In addition, I needed to spend time with Keith to learn the offense and terminology, as well as meet the offensive linemen I would be coaching and get to know them. I began working the lists and making calls.

When camp began in July, the temperature in Hattiesburg was 105 degrees. I was slowly adjusting to the heat. We made our final playbook adjustments and got organized for the players to report in August. Two-a-day practices were quickly on us. I learned our personnel and began getting them ready for the season-opener.

Each Thursday we had a recruiting meeting where we commented on recruits from our areas. Of course, I didn't have as much information as the other coaches because I had missed the May recruiting period. I had several names on my list. Brett Favre's wasn't among them.

 **Fact 4 Favre**

Brett Favre played quarterback, safety and also served as the punter and placekicker for Hancock North Central.

Coaches hit the road after practice on Thursday to visit high schools on Friday. That's when we developed a rapport with the high school coaches and tried to sell our university and our program. My first Friday out, I visited schools between Hattiesburg and the Gulf Coast. There were plenty of good players and programs in the area and I enjoyed working it. I visited coaches and inquired about the players we liked. I then asked for game tapes and then determined whether I would write an evaluation or scratch the player from my list. My job was to whittle the list from 75 to 30, realizing that maybe seven or eight would actually visit our campus.

I talked with several coaches along the Gulf Coast and one coach asked if I had seen the quarterback from Hancock North Central. I asked his name and was told, "Brett Favre." I remembered the name of the school more than the name of the player. I figured the coach who had worked the area before me had evaluated Brett and determined he couldn't play at Southern Miss, so I gave it little thought. Brett's name came up again at another school, then again and again. I was curious.

(Photo by Beverly McHale)

The stands at Hancock North Central High School haven't changed much in the 20 years since Mark McHale sat there the first time to watch Brett Favre play. Favre wasn't on McHale's recruiting list until a couple of high school coaches in southern Mississippi suggested he visit the school.

I asked for the head coach's name at Hancock North Central and was told it was Irvin Favre. I called Coach Favre and told him I'd like to visit him.

I made Hancock North Central my last visit, as I wanted to hit my other schools where I knew I had prospects. I figured seeing Coach Favre would be nothing more than a social visit anyway. I followed the directions I had been given and wondered where a high school could be in this setting. As I came upon the school, I wondered if I had made a wrong turn. There was a school, but it looked like an elementary.

Across the road, though, was a football field, the home of the Hancock North Central Hawks. The Rose Bowl it wasn't. A small set of bleachers that might have seated 500 people sat on the home side, with a smaller set across the field for the visitors. The press box was tiny, with just enough room for the scoreboard operator and one or two other people to film the games or keep statistics. A wooden ticket booth and a metal building were the only other structures.

As I parked my car, I thought I was on a wild goose chase. I thought, "what am I doing here?" It was about 10 to 4 and school had dismissed, leaving few cars on the parking lot. I headed for the metal building at the end of the field, looking for Coach Favre. After poking around I found him and he told me to "come on in and have a seat." The only place to sit was one of those vinyl couches with a split in the middle and foam sticking out. Irvin was at a wooden desk covered with notebooks, playbooks and all kinds of other things. On the wall was a mass-produced cardboard schedule. I studied it to see if Hancock North Central played any of the teams on my master list. It didn't. A small TV sat on a table with wheels, and video tapes were on top of it, under it and on the floor.

Irvin and I swapped small talk for a few minutes and he told me he had played baseball on scholarship at Southern Miss. I figured what I had here was a Southern Miss graduate who thinks he has a player capable of playing at his alma mater. I asked Irvin about a player he had that was supposed to be pretty good. I added that I was new on staff and didn't know the area well, yet, but that I had a master list and his player's name wasn't on it. Irvin told me the previous recruiter came through and didn't see practice nor watch film but promised to follow up in the fall.

(Favre family photo)

Brett Favre and high school sweetheart Deanna at their prom. They later became husband and wife.

I pulled out a notebook and asked Irvin to spell the young quarterback's name. Irvin said, "B-r-e-t-t F-a-v-r-e." I said, "Irvin, you and your quarterback have the same last name. You wouldn't be related would you?" Irvin glanced at me with a puppy dog look and said, "you know Coach McHale, Brett is my son."

It didn't take long for me to determine that this wasn't good. Here was a head coach who was a Southern Miss alum whose son was the quarterback. I figured next I'd get the good ole speech, "he can play for you even though he's my son." Sure enough, that's what Irvin said.

A lot of coaches place their sons at quarterback because it's the most important position on the field. Most of the time the kid isn't a true quarterback. I asked Irvin if he had any tapes on Brett. Irvin hollered to an assistant in the other room, "do we have any tapes on Brett from this year?" The coach found a couple and brought them in. Irvin filtered through some tapes around the TV to see if he had more. He popped in

17

Mark McHale met Irvin Favre in the field house at Hancock North Central more to introduce himself to the coach than to recruit the coach's quarterback/son.

a tape and pointed out Brett to me.

"That's him wearing number 10 in the white jersey," Irvin said, adding that Brett also played free safety on defense. As I watched the tape I saw an average, slow, white boy hand off the ball to a running back play after play. When Brett was on defense I never could see him because of the angle of the camera and because it was zoomed in too close on each play.

It must have been the third quarter before I saw Brett throw a pass on that tape. He threw maybe two play-action passes. One was a short completion. The receiver dropped the other one. I asked Irvin if he had any more tapes.

"I don't have any more," Irvin said. "They must all be mailed out to other colleges so they could evaluate Brett."

I told Irvin that for me to evaluate Brett as a Division I quarterback I had to see tapes of him throwing the ball. If I took the tape I had just watched to Southern Miss, Brett definitely would get turned down for a scholarship. I'm sure the coach who came to HNC in the spring observed the same thing and thought Brett wasn't a prospect, and rightfully so. I asked Irvin for some tapes of Brett as a junior. Irvin found a few and I fast forwarded through them until I found Brett throwing passes. I studied his throwing motion, arm strength and accuracy. He didn't throw a lot, making him difficult to evaluate, so I ran some of the passes in slow motion to get a better look.

After I watched the tapes, Irvin asked what I thought.

"Does Brett have a chance?," Irvin asked.

"Very honestly, what little footage I could see of Brett throwing the ball, I thought he had some talent," I said.

"I've watched him since he was a little kid and I'm telling you he can sling that football," Irvin said.

We visited a little more and Irvin walked with me to my car. Irvin anxiously asked if I could come to Hancock North Central's game next Friday.

"You could get a good look at Brett throwing the ball in that game," Irvin said.

I told Irvin I had a lot of recruiting to do, official visits to set up, a master list to shorten and a lot of evaluating to do on top of everything else. Irvin kept pleading, promising to throw the ball and that I wouldn't be sorry. I didn't promise Irvin anything, but I told him I'd try to organize my trip next week to see Brett play. I didn't want to upset an alumnus.

As I was getting into my car, a thin, blond-haired kid jogged around the corner of the field house. Irvin introduced me to him. My first impression of Brett was one of complete confidence. He was big-eyed and full of energy.

"Coach McHale, I can play for you and I want to go to Southern Mississippi," Brett said.

I told Brett that because of NCAA rules I wasn't allowed to speak with him and that I would come see him play.

"That's great," Brett said. "You won't be sorry you did."

Irvin still was working me.

"What if you came by and Brett just happened to be throwing the ball on the field," Irvin said. "Could you watch him then?"

I told Irvin it would have to be during our open date and it would have to be a complete coincidence. I could see the wheels turning in Irvin's mind.

I left, hurrying off to the Gulf Coast to grab a bite to eat and to watch the halves of two different games. As I drove away, I tried to evaluate the whole situation. I liked Brett's arm on tape. His dad was a good salesman and Brett had a certain air about him, a mix of cockiness and confidence I like to see in a quarterback. I made up my mind to watch him play a game.

The next week I added Brett's name to the master list. Our staff met again to go over the names. Each coach would say something meaningful about the players on this list. They'd mention who else was offering scholarships to their prospects. Some of them we were offering, too. Others were getting scratched off the list. When it came to my list, I talked about Brett and told the staff I was going to watch him play before I decided whether Keith should watch him on film.

On Friday, I called Irvin to tell him I was coming to see Brett play and stressed how important it was to see him throw the ball. Irvin obviously was excited and said, "You bet! Come by at 7:30 for the kickoff."

I got there a little before 7 p.m. and went to see Irvin while his players stretched. I wanted to make sure he knew I was there and I wanted to emphasize how important it was that Brett throw. I shook Irvin's hand, wished him luck and headed to the bleachers to get a seat. It wasn't hard to find a place. I walked right up to the 50-yard line and got a seat at the top of the bleachers. A group of Hancock players came onto the field. I spotted No. 10. He was bigger than the center snapping the ball to him.

I knew all quarterbacks threw the ball in pre-game warmups, even if they didn't plan to throw much during the game. I hoped to see for myself then and there what kind of arm Brett had. He started out throwing from a three-step drop. The receivers went downfield six yards and broke out. Brett's throws were crisp, on target and had a perfect spiral. The receivers dropped most of them. He threw the out cut like it was his deepest ball — hard. He progressed to throwing to his backs and I noticed the same thing. They were having trouble catching the ball. It was obvious Brett didn't have what coaches call a grading mechanism. A grading mechanism is controlling the velocity of the ball, having a soft touch on short passes and throwing harder on deeper routes.

Brett started throwing some deep balls. It was unbelievable! He could throw it deep and it had smoke on it. His throws were pretty, with the right arc and nose path. I was impressed. Very impressed.

As the Hancock North team jogged off the field, I watched the opponents continue to warm up. The contrast in Brett's ability and that of the opposing quarterback was dramatic. I started to think I had stumbled onto the best-kept secret in football. I was eager to see Brett throw in a game situation.

"You must be Coach McHale," said a lady who sat down next to me, noticing the Southern Miss logo on my shirt.

I told her I was and asked who she might be.

"I'm Bonita Favre, Irvin's wife, and my son is number 10, the quarterback."

I apologetically told Bonita that NCAA rules prohibited me from talking with parents during a game. She understood, but I was always uncomfortable telling parents that. I was afraid it made the parents think I wasn't very friendly. It seems like a silly rule.

Hancock North received the opening kickoff and Brett led the offense on the field. The first play was a run up the middle. It was a harbinger of things to come. Everything was Brett handing the ball off to a running back, other than a couple of plays where Brett ran the ball himself on the option. He was no Reggie Collier, but he did have a presence about him and obviously was in control.

Brett played free safety on defense, but most of the plays were stopped before he could make a tackle, so I couldn't get much of a read on his ability there. He did make a couple of tackles and looked more like a linebacker, showing toughness usually not associated with quarterbacks.

I was frustrated that I had sacrificed a night to see Brett play and he wasn't throwing the ball. Finally, just before halftime, Brett faked a handoff and threw a short pass to his running back. At least Brett didn't knock him over the way he did in warmups. Hancock

Fact 4 Favre

Brett Favre grew up idolizing former New Orleans Saints quarterback Archie Manning and former Dallas Cowboys quarterback Roger Staubach.

North drove to the 5-yard line and Brett faked another run and threw a touchdown pass to a wide receiver.

During the first half, a group of people were getting all over Irvin. They were giving him a hard time and Bonita was right in the middle of them. I found that quite entertaining. Later I found out that the folks yelling were relatives. That's something you don't see every day.

I had planned to leave at halftime and catch the second half of another game to evaluate another prospect but I needed to see more of Brett. Through the years, Irvin had won a lot of games running the ball. Maybe he was waiting to get a big lead before letting Brett throw. At least that's the reasoning I used to talk myself into sticking around for the second half.

Brett threw one more pass and it was incomplete.

Hancock won convincingly, but I didn't get to see what I needed for a true evaluation. As I was leaving the bleachers, Bonita asked me what I thought. I told her he needed to throw more to get evaluated. Irvin asked me the same question, his chest sticking out full of pride as if I'd

Hancock North Central isn't much different than it was when Brett Favre was a student athlete there in the mid-1980s.

(Photos by Beverly McHale)

seen something that would cause me to offer Brett a scholarship on the spot. I told Irvin that if I took a tape of this game back to Southern Miss, Brett wouldn't be considered for a scholarship. I explained that our quarterback coach needed to see Brett's throwing ability.

"Coach McHale, if you come back next week, I promise to throw the ball more," Irvin said, some desperation creeping into his words. "I'll do whatever it takes to get him a scholarship. I promise!"

I explained to Irvin that I couldn't promise anything. Recruiting time is precious and I had to get to the New Orleans area to see some games there. Irvin persisted, practically begging me to come back. I told Irvin I'd have to see if I could work it out, but that probably I would just have to get a tape of a later game.

I knew Irvin was disappointed. I was really disappointed. I wondered if I had wasted a night of recruiting watching just an average high school player. As I drove back to Hattiesburg I thought about several of the prospects I'd seen on tape and of some I had yet to see in person.

My thoughts, though, wandered back to Brett during warmups. He had a good arm. I decided then and there to hang in there with him. I had a gut feeling I needed to see him one more time.

At our Thursday recruiting meeting, we went through all the names on our list. We were scratching a lot of players and some were scratching us. I talked Brett up a little bit, mentioning his toughness, size and arm. I mentioned that he could play defense if he didn't work out at quarterback. I had to stop short, though. I needed one more good look at Brett before I could recommend him to Keith as a legitimate quarterback prospect.

We played road games for the next two weeks, so I couldn't see Brett play. Fortunately, one of those games was at Tulane, which allowed me the chance to scout my prospects in the New Orleans area before rejoining our team for the game on Saturday. That allowed me to schedule one more visit to Hancock North , about eight weeks into the season. I called Irvin to let him know I was coming and he assured me he would have Brett throw the ball more.

I got to the field early again so I could see Brett throw in warmups again. Brett had twice as strong an arm as any other quarterback I was evaluating. I just hoped that this time I got to see it in a live game situation.

This game progressed much like the first time I saw Brett. He threw four passes in the first half. One was an impressive 20-yarder over the middle. The other three were short. Two were caught and one was dropped. I was frustrated. I still hadn't seen enough of Brett to recommend him. I decided to stay for the second half because there were no other games in my area close enough for me to get to in time.

The second half began with Hancock North with the ball at midfield. Brett handed off on the first play and I thought, "here we go again." On the next play, Brett faked a handoff out of the I-formation, hid the ball well and set up for a pass. He was looking to throw the ball deep, but the receiver was covered. His protection collapsed and Brett scrambled to his right. The little receiver on the right side cut across the field to the left hash area into the end zone. Brett set his feet on the right hash, drew back his arm and unloaded a rocket. That ball had flames and smoke coming off it. The little receiver caught it and I could hear the crack as the ball made contact with the breastplate of his shoulder pads. I don't know how he hung onto the ball, but he did.

I was astonished! Now, I was convinced Brett was for real. The important thing Brett had shown was that he had not only a good arm, but a big-time arm. That's a great place to start if you're recruiting a quarterback. I had seen Shane Matthews play at Pascagoula (Miss.) High School. Shane threw a lot and put up big statistics. He broke Steve Spurrier's records at the University of Florida, but his arm wasn't even close to Brett's.

After Brett drilled that little receiver, he got excited, jumped up and down and raised both arms signaling a touchdown, then sprinted to the receiver and hugged him. Here was a young man who loved playing football. I could tell he was having fun and that presence he had about him was more evident than ever.

Brett threw a couple of more short passes that night, but I had seen enough. I saw Irvin after the game and I was excited, but I had to temper it.

"Well, what do you think," Irvin asked.

I told Irvin that Brett still needed to throw more to get evaluated but that I would do everything I could to get him a scholarship at Southern Miss. Irvin grinned from ear to ear and said, "Coach, he can play for Southern. I know he can!"

> **"I'm telling you: open your eyes and look at the fields, for they are ready for the harvest." – John 4:35.**

BRETT'S VIEW

How much knowledge did I have about the recruiting process? None.

I didn't know that a coach had a particular area or region that he covered. I thought it all was just kind of by word of mouth, which in some respects it is. Kind of a, "Hey, come look at my boy," kind of thing.

Now, I realize that a coach has a lot of schools to cover and it's easy to pass up a guy who might be a hidden gem. A coach can get blinded by statistics or by a guy who plays at a bigger school. It's no different in college when NFL scouts are looking for players. You hear about the teams that are on TV all the time. I can see how a kid from Hancock North Central High School or at one of those other schools like that doesn't get much recognition or gets overlooked. It's amazing how much film a coach has to watch and how many man hours he has to drive to and from, how much he's on the phone and all that stuff.

I didn't know how important a player's junior year of high school was. I figured you could stink it up or light it up as a junior and it didn't really matter. I didn't know and Dad didn't really tell me much. I'd hear that two people from Tulane were coming. They could have been secretaries for all I knew. I didn't really know if anyone was coming.

I didn't know what recruiters wanted to see. If I threw the ball six times in a game, that was pretty good. That was a lot. We just didn't throw the ball. When I realized that Coach McHale wanted to see me throw the ball, I had to make it good. One completion per game for 60 yards wasn't uncommon, but I had to make it good, so even if I didn't complete them I had to throw them pretty good. They had to be dazzling, I guess is a good way to put it. It might only be one or two plays a game because we weren't going to throw 30 times. I wanted any coach watching me to leave saying, "he only threw two but one of them was to his left and 80 yards back to the right. I always was thinking something like that."

I remember the first time Coach McHale came to talk to me. I thought I could do just about everything. I always thought it was going to work out. That was my mentality. Dad kept me humble, though. We rode home together like we always did and it was always an interesting ride. He made me put about 75 cents of regular gasoline in the truck. He was a tight wad, now. He'd scrounge up whatever

(Favre family photo)

Bonita and Irvin worked at Benny French's Tavern in addition to their teaching and coaching jobs. The bar's pool tables and pinball machines became toys for Scott and Brett when they were youngsters since the family had living quarters in the back of the establishment.

change he had. He'd look under the seat and find four or five pennies, three dimes and a couple of nickels and make me go in the Magic Market. He thought by doing it that way he wouldn't have to put $20 in the tank. He figured if he put just enough in to get us home and back to school the next day he was saving money.

For a while, Mom and Dad had a job in a bar. They cleaned up and tended bar a little and slept on a mattress on the floor. There was a curtain they pulled that blocked off where they stayed from the rest of the bar. One night two guys got into a fist fight and came flying through that curtain as they were getting ready for school.

For a while we practically grew up in that bar. School teachers in Mississippi don't make a whole lot of money. Dad, being a coach, didn't make much extra money. They're married, working in that bar and going to school. My brother Scott and I could barely see over the pool table, but we'd be in there hobnobbing with the rest of them. It was just a way of life to us.

It was a big place with a lot of people. There were all those video games, pinball, air hockey and stuff. Scott and I would go back there in the back and drink about 10 of those little 8-ounce Cokes, get sick eating Kit Kats and sandwiches. We'd steal rolls of quarters to play all those games. We'd steal pool balls off the table. We'd sneak a little drink of Dixie Beer from the back. Oh man. We just blended right in. My grandmother had a little trailer out back. We stayed there a lot, too. Our house was 23 or 24 miles from there. I remember staying at our house and at that bar.

Later on when we'd drive home from school, Dad would scrape together some money for gas and I'd say, "hey Dad, how about a root beer."

He'd say, "I'll root beer your ass. You go in there and pay for the gas." I was a senior in high school. It wasn't like I was in sixth grade.

On the way home, all the time it was about football and baseball. Other kids were out doing other things. I was doing sports and if I wasn't doing them I was talking about them or doing push-ups or sit-ups.

"We were playing some kind of sport all the time," Scott Favre said. "We would play out in the yard. Football, baseball, whatever. We were really competitive with one another and that made both of us better and we had a lot of fun. We'd see who could throw the hardest. If it was raining, we'd go in the old barn and play football indoors. I remember one time Brett threw a pass too close to the house and I leaned out to get it and went through the window. We were always into something."

Chapter 4

Post-season recruiting

The next week at our recruiting meeting I couldn't wait to brag on this recruit I stumbled on in Kiln, Miss. Brag I did. Coach Carmody kept asking how fast Brett was. I told him Brett had deceiving speed and he was hard to tackle because he knew how to avoid straight hits, but he wasn't a speedster.

What kind of offense were we running? What kind of quarterback was running it? The option, where the quarterback's speed and athleticism were the No. 1 priority. Brett was no Reggie Collier. How in the world was I going to sell this quarterback to our offensive coordinator who was looking for an option quarterback? It was going to be incredibly difficult.

 **Fact 4 Favre**

Hancock North Central High School retired Brett Favre's No. 10 in 1993.

Our season ended and we had a winning record, but we took it on the chin from the top programs on our schedule. Reggie Colliers come along once in a great while and we didn't have one this season. When we got behind Florida State and Alabama, it was hard to get back in the game. We didn't have the passing attack to complement the option. I was convinced we needed a drop-back passer if we were going to compete with the top teams on our schedule.

If we continued with the option, played tough defense, were strong on special teams and controlled the ball, we could have winning seasons. To beat the better teams, the powerhouses, we needed a great passer. I was convinced Brett was that quarterback. All I had to do was get him a scholarship and get him on campus. When our staff saw Brett's arm, he would have to play and we would have to change our offense. Selling Brett to our staff was going to be tough, though, and it was going to take a great deal of patience on everyone's part.

Our next phase of recruiting after the May period was to get scholarship approvals for players not already approved. That meant bringing back game tapes to our campus for the position coach and head coach to approve them.

As I made my recruiting rounds, visiting players and their parents, setting up their official visits to our campus and watching some of them play basketball, I stopped by to see Irvin and Brett. Irvin was in his office and Brett hadn't arrived, yet. I told Irvin I needed as many game tapes as I could get to take back so Keith Daniels could evaluate Brett. Irvin had just three tapes and none were from the games I had seen in person. I told Irvin I really needed those two tapes.

"They're all out," Irvin said. "Delta State, Pearl River Junior College and some other schools are looking at them. Coach, they have to look at Brett in case he doesn't get a scholarship from Southern Miss. No other Division I school is talking to Brett."

At 10 to 4, Brett walked into the office at the end of the conversation. I explained the recruiting process to Brett and told him where he stood. Brett had just finished lifting weights and was showing me his biceps. His favorite words were, "Coach, I can play for you!" I wasn't sure if Brett really understood the process of recruiting. Most of our prospects had already been to Hattiesburg to see a game, had talked frequently with our head coach, had received a home visit from an assistant coach and maybe even a home visit from the head coach. A date for an official visit to our campus had been set up for them, as well. All Brett had received was a couple of visits to his school by assistant coaches and only one, mine, was from a Division I school.

I told Brett I believed in him, but it wasn't up to me alone. I needed to get him approved by our quarterbacks coach and maybe even by our defensive coaches, in case he played safety, before I could offer a scholarship. I told him to be patient until we could look at the tapes. Brett understood.

"I'll be looking forward to hearing from you," Brett said. "Thanks for coming by to tell me this. I'd much rather play for Southern Miss than go to a junior college or a small school. I know I can play for you. I'm sure of it!"

I took the tapes back to Keith and explained that Brett's team didn't throw often, so in order to get a fair evaluation he needed to watch all three. I was a little nervous because I knew what Keith was looking for in an option quarterback, but I thought maybe he would see Brett's outstanding arm and would overlook a few things.

I finished looking at the offensive line tapes I had been given and went to Keith's office to see what he thought of Brett. I asked if he had a chance to look at all three tapes.

"I sure did," Keith said.

Naturally, I asked what he thought.

Keith was polite and gently answered, "he can't play for us Mark. He looks too slow on film. I'm not sure about his throwing ability because there weren't too many passes on the tapes I looked at and the only passes I got to see were short."

I took those tapes back to my office and watched them again. Keith was right. On these tapes, there was no way to gauge Brett's athletic ability. Keith figured any quarterback who just handed off and didn't throw much was no better than an average high school athlete or the coach would use his running and throwing ability more.

For a prospect to make "the board," that is the recruiting board, he had to be approved after we had seen him on tape. Making the board didn't guarantee a scholarship, but the player was listed by priority under the position he was to play in college. We had a magnetic name tag of each player we felt might be worthy of a scholarship. The players were arranged in order of preference. On our board were 13 quarterbacks and we were going to sign just two. Brett's name was not on the board. That meant we wouldn't be discussing him.

Each weekend, for various reasons, we removed names from the board. Less often, we added names to the board after those players received a good evaluation after we reviewed their tapes.

I went back out to visit my prospects and pick up more tapes. I went to see Irvin and Brett. Irvin was eager to hear what our staff thought and we talked a long time. Irvin knew I was on Brett's side. I told him we were going to have to be very patient. I told Irvin I needed a copy of every tape he had of Brett and I needed them in the next two weeks. We had to let Keith see every pass Brett had thrown. Irvin pledged to get it done and he did.

In the meantime, I was making a big recruiting push with Chris Ryals, a 6-foot-7, 300-pound offensive lineman from Purvis, Miss., about 13 miles from Hattiesburg. Chris' dad played at Southern Miss, which might have given us an edge on Mississippi State, which was recruiting Chris hard. Chris was a very likeable kid. Little did I know how that would come into play.

I took Brett's tapes back to Keith, just trying to get Brett's name on the board. Every chance I got, I bragged about Brett to our head coach. Coach Carmody told me three different alumni had called him about Brett. He told me to "get him approved on tape."

Hancock North Central dedicated its football field to Brett Favre in 2004 with this statue and plaque outside the facility, which is now named "Brett Favre Field."

Brett Lorenzo Favre

One of the greatest quarterbacks and football players of all time. Brett was three year starter for Hancock High and played in the Mississippi High School All Star Football Game. His jersey #10 was retired in April 1993.

He was a four year starting quarterback at U.S.M. During that time he led h team to 29 victories and two bowl triumphs, and finished as the school's a time leading passer. His jersey #4 was retired in September 1993.

Selected in the second round by Atlanta in the 1991 NFL draft, Favre was traded in 1992 to Green Bay, where he became the NFL's only three-time M\ Favre led the Packers to multiple division titles, NFC Championship games and Super Bowls, including a victory in Super Bowl XXXI. A perennial Pro Bowl selection, he ranks in the league's top five in career victories, touchdown passes, passing yards, completions, and attempts and holds th league record for most consecutive starts by a quarterback.

"The good Lord gave you a body that can stand most anything.
It's your mind you have to convince." - Vince Lombardi

Dedicated May 8, 2004

(Photos by Beverly McHale)

A lot was going on with our program. Keith was getting hassled by some alumni about our option offense. They thought we should throw more and Keith was getting tired of the nagging. Mississippi had an opening for a quarterback coach and that week they called Keith. Coach Carmody was very loyal to his assistants and he told Keith he wanted him to stay. He encouraged Keith to ignore the fans and that he was pleased with the offense. Keith went up to Oxford to talk to Ole Miss that weekend, so I kept Brett's tapes to myself until I knew what Keith was going to do. That meant no one saw the tapes that weekend.

I drove back to Kiln to tell Irvin what was going on. Irvin was getting nervous. He said Delta State was trying to get Brett to commit there. Irvin said Delta State coaches told him if Brett didn't commit soon, they would give the scholarship to another quarterback. I told Irvin Delta State was bluffing and that the scholarship would still be there. It was 10 to 4 when Bonita walked in. It was the first time I had a chance to talk to her about Brett's status. Irvin and Bonita were afraid of missing out on a scholarship, and paying for Brett to go to college would be expensive for a couple with teachers' salaries.

This was late in the recruiting process. Our head coach was making visits and prospects were coming to our campus. Brett hadn't even been offered a scholarship to Southern Miss. There was no reason for Coach Carmody to visit him. Time was running short.

I came back to Southern Miss to find that Keith had taken the job at Ole Miss. Coach Carmody told us wide receivers coach Jack White, the guy who had picked me up at the airport, would be our new offensive coordinator and quarterbacks coach. It clicked in my head that Brett might have a better chance at a scholarship. Jack was from California and had been coaching at Oregon before coming to Southern Miss. The pass-oriented West Coast offense was just getting cranked up. Jack's background was anything but the option. This could change the whole outlook on this slow country boy from Kiln.

> **"Keep asking, and it will be given to you. Keep searching, and you will find. Keep knocking, and the door will be opened to you."**
> **– Matthew 7:7.**

BRETT'S VIEW

I remember Coach McHale and my dad really hit it off. I knew that didn't guarantee me a scholarship, but it did kind of spark an interest.

We knew we'd gotten to Coach McHale and we had to keep it going. We knew he was interested and that he would come back because there was a relationship there. Still, I didn't know a lot about what was going on.

I remember dad talking about we had to do whatever we could to get me a scholarship. I remember thinking, "Throw the dang ball!"

A few other coaches came by and said they couldn't recruit me. Half of them probably are out of coaching, now. Some of the schools probably sent some of the old bald coaches and stuff to see me.

Mom kind of stayed out of it, other than telling Dad to throw the dang ball or he'd be paying for me to go school. I can hear her now. Dad told me when Coach McHale was coming in from Southern Miss and I don't know that that created any added pressure. I wanted to do well anyway. Throwing three or four times a game, there were two ways to look at it. One was that I had better make those three or four passes count, which created a lot of pressure. The other way to look at it was that with just three or four passes per game, I couldn't do enough to impress or not impress anyone.

I looked at the intangibles — blocking and tackling because I played both ways. I knew I could throw and that Coach McHale wasn't going to get to see me throw a lot of precision routes and things like that, but he knew I could throw it out of the stadium. So that was my way of going about it. I knew I had touch on my passes, but I wasn't going to worry about that. Anyone can have touch. I wanted to show I could do something nobody else could do.

I didn't think a lot about any college scout coming in. I think I was different. If I thought about it too much, then I couldn't get on the field quickly enough to show what I could do. I was like that in baseball, too. If a baseball scout was going to be there, I couldn't wait to go out and field ground balls or take batting practice or actually make a cold throw from shortstop.

Having a scout in the stands watching me, I compare that to when Deanna and I first started dating. I'd be pitching in a baseball game and after every pitch I'd look over there to see if she was looking. Of course she was looking, but I wanted to make sure, you know, that she wasn't over there talking to some boy or something. I wanted to make sure I was getting all of her attention.

It was no different when a scout would come to watch me play in college. There are plays where I was aware I was being watched and there were plays where I'd just forget about it. For the most part, in high school, I wanted to make sure Coach McHale was looking.

I wasn't so much worried about throwing the ball a lot so the recruiters could see me. I talked with Dad about throwing the ball more just because I wanted to do it. I thought what we were doing still was enough to get me recruited. When I look back, that's true but if I had put up 3,000 yards and 30 touchdowns there might have been more recruiters calling. Then again, it might not have worked out the way that it did. I was just being kind of selfish. I just wanted to throw, but we were pretty good running the ball.

When I knew Coach McHale was coming to see me I talked to Dad about throwing more. We butted heads a little bit, but really it was no different than any other time. I'd tell Dad if I thought a certain play wasn't working and that hasn't changed throughout my career.

When Dad evaluated the film, he always was harder on me than on the other guys, but I was rebellious to a certain degree and he'd put me in my place. I had a blast doing what we did. We were running the ball and running the option and when I did throw it wasn't the old five-step drop. I thought I was doing enough to get noticed. It was just that occasionally I wanted to do this or that.

Still, I felt my throwing ability was my best asset and that was the thing we were using the least. I thought that was backwards. I wanted to show everyone that I could do everything else, too. I wanted to show I could run, block, tackle, punt, all that. I thought I was pretty good at running the ball. I couldn't do it now, but at the time I thought it showed my versatility. Looking back, throwing more probably would have sparked more interest in me, but it worked out fine.

I think Dad never wanted me to think that my getting a scholarship was more important than the team. He got a lot of heat anyway. Changing the offense for me would open him up to the criticism that he was just doing it because he wanted to get his son a scholarship, which obviously wasn't true. If he was trying to get me a scholarship, he'd have thrown the ball 40 times a game.

The way Dad coached me and taught me, he showed me that the team was more important than any one player. My family always gave Dad a hard time.

It's no easy trek to the Favre home on Irvin Favre Road. The house sits on the now-famous Rotten Bayou in southern Mississippi.

(Photos by Beverly McHale)

Chapter 5

Film approval

I asked Jack what kind of offense we were gong to run and he told me he wasn't sure, but it wouldn't be the option and he was going to add some drop-back passing. I told Jack I had a quarterback in my area who had the best arm I'd ever seen. I told Jack he needed to look at Brett on tape before we went out recruiting again. Jack agreed and I came back with 10 tapes.

"Wow," Jack said. "What is all that?"

I told Jack he needed to look at every tape and fast forward to the passes. I knew that would be pure misery, especially for a coach with a bunch of other tapes to watch. I guess in all the excitement of Jack getting his promotion and all the people coming by to congratulate him, I had caught him at just the ideal moment because he agreed.

When I checked back in with Jack, he told me he had watched some, but not all, of the tapes, which was all right because they were copies for us to keep and I didn't have to return them to Irvin.

When I asked Jack what he thought, he

(Photo by Beverly McHale)

The Favre home on Rotten Bayou was at the end of Irvin Favre Road. Mark McHale discovered on his travels through the South it's not uncommon for a road to be named for a family that lives on it.

hesitated a bit. I thought that wasn't a good sign. Being the new coordinator, he didn't want to start out by hurting someone's feelings.

35

A new coordinator always wants to start out on the right foot with his position coaches.

Jack diplomatically said, "he does a lot of things I like. Let's not scratch him from the list. I'll look at those other tapes later."

I knew I had one foot in the door. I decided to try to get the other one in while I had the opportunity. I suggested we put Brett's name on the board so we could discuss him at our next meeting. Jack looked a bit puzzled but agreed. I was walking on air. I couldn't wait to tell Irvin and Brett. I called them and set up a visit for the following week. I met with Irvin at his office. I noticed the time. It was 10 to 4.

We left to go to the family home on Irvin Favre Road. I found that interesting. Where I came from, you had to be a president, have gotten shot or something like that to have a road named for you. I learned later that in Mississippi nearly everyone in the county has a road named after him. It had something to do with the fire department and emergency system.

When we arrived at the house, I met Brett's brothers Scott and Jeff, along with his sister Brandi. Bonita gave me a tour of the house and showed me the boys' room and all their trophies from their days playing sports. Irvin took me outside and showed me the homestead, which sat on Rotten Bayou, and gave me a little history

> ### 🏈 Fact 4 Favre
>
> Brett Favre holds or shares six career records at Southern Mississippi:
> 1. Plays (1,362)
> 2. Total offense (7,606)
> 3. Passing yards (7,695)
> 4. Completions (613)
> 5. Pass attempts (1,169)
> 6. Touchdowns (52, tied with Lee Roberts)

of the area. We went inside to discuss the status of a scholarship. I excitedly told the family that Brett had made the recruiting board. Obviously, I was more excited than they were because they asked what that meant.

I explained what the recruiting board was. I told them about Keith going to Ole Miss and Jack coming from Oregon. I explained how our change in offensive coordinators aided Brett's chances and then I fielded their questions. Bonita wanted to know if Brett's addition to the recruiting board and the change in offensive coordinators meant that he was going to get a scholarship. She was eager and rightfully so. Paying a youngster's way to college on teachers' salaries wouldn't be easy. She peppered me with questions about whether the family would visit the school and such. I tried to answer everything as she asked without making any promises I couldn't keep.

I explained in detail that essentially it boiled down to the fact that we had gone from a week ago Brett having zero chance of landing a scholarship to this week having a pretty good chance. They didn't know that at one point Brett's chances appeared over for good. They kept hoping and their hope appeared as if it at least had an outside chance of being rewarded.

I asked for more patience, a difficult request being that we all knew time was running short. If the family invested in the hopes of Brett receiving a scholarship to Southern Miss and that scholarship never materialized, what would they do? Would Brett go to college to play football at all?

The Favres really wanted Brett to go to a NCAA Division I college, but by putting all their eggs in that basket, they felt they risked him not being able to go anywhere else. This was a nerve-wracking gamble on their part and I certainly didn't want to let them down.

Irvin and Bonita really wanted Brett to go to Southern Miss. Irvin told me a decision had to be made pretty soon because Delta State had kind of come into the picture and was going to offer Brett a scholarship but if he didn't take it, they would pull the offer and give it to someone else. I think Irvin was testing the waters to see how serious Southern Miss was.

I never ever saw another recruiter at Brett's house, his school or a game. In all my years of recruiting, that never had happened before. You run into recruiters going in and out the door all the time. Sometimes there are two or three recruiters in a school's office waiting to see a guy. I never saw anybody from Delta State. Maybe Delta State had shown some interest, but, in reality, Brett had no scholarship offers at all.

> **"Rejoice always! Pray constantly. Give thanks in everything, for this is God's will for you in Christ Jesus."**
> **– I Thessalonians 5:16-18.**

BRETT'S VIEW

It was late in my senior year and I didn't have one Division I scholarship offer. Yeah, it was disappointing. I probably was no different than a lot of guys. I really felt I was deserving of a scholarship, but my thoughts started turning to, "well maybe if I had thrown more." But I knew our offense wasn't built around that, so I figured, "oh well

37

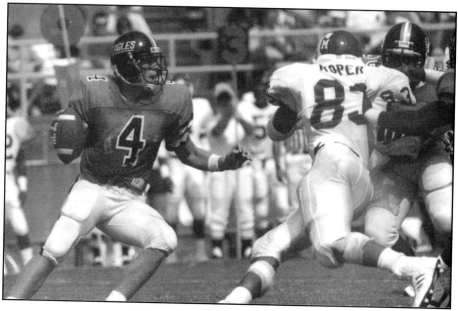

(University of Southern Mississippi photo)

Brett Favre had hopes of playing for Southern Mississippi after making numerous visits to games early in his high school career.

that's just the way it is."

I figured I'd just have to go to a junior college or something and prove I was worth a scholarship. I wasn't so much disappointed. I never thought that it was because I wasn't good enough. I felt like it was just our type of offense and that's the way it was. It wasn't like I threw a lot and wasn't very good at it. It was kind of the stuff coaches didn't see. I could just hear recruiters telling Dad that they didn't get to see his son do enough of this or enough of that. I wasn't disappointed in that and I wasn't mad at Dad. I just thought I'd have to prove myself another way.

I could have changed the way I did things, but that wouldn't have been right. I played the same way I've always played throughout my career. I never thought twice about it. I just tried to play well. I played the only way I know how. I never threw in the towel because I wasn't getting recruited. I just played the same way.

Dad and I talked a little about recruiting, but we never had arguments. I never said to him that if we'd thrown the ball more I'd have gotten a scholarship. In fact, we joked more about that after the fact than we ever talked about it before. Heck, I thought I was just doing what Dad asked me to do. I thought I was doing plenty well enough. I might not have been throwing it 20 or 30 times a game, but there was no one who could throw it like me.

I wasn't aware of anyone from Delta State. I never remember seeing anyone from Delta State at all. I can see why Dad would say that. I don't know if anyone ever came by from Delta State. Dad might have been pulling (Coach McHale's) leg. To me, it was like we'll hold out for Southern Miss until the end and if that doesn't work out then we'll look at Delta State. I'd just go play there or at Pearl River Junior College.

I remember Coach McHale coming back a bunch, but it wasn't that far away from Hattiesburg, so I didn't look at it as a special trip. I didn't have any idea how it all worked. I didn't know the offensive coordinator looked at the tapes. I thought it was the head coach or the staff sat around and watched them together as a group.

After Coach McHale took the tapes back to Southern Miss, I remember Dad telling me my chances didn't look good.

I remember going to some Southern Miss games when I was younger, but not on a recruiting trip. I went up for a game my senior year. Ailrick Young was the quarterback. I remember they ran the option but I wasn't in a position to pick whether I wanted to go to a school that ran the ball or one that threw it. I just wanted to play. I thought I could run the option. Looking back, I probably couldn't have at that level. I could get by, but I couldn't run like some of those guys.

(University of Southern Mississippi photo)

Brett Favre knew he faced long odds when it came to his college recruiting.

I was aware that the odds were against me even if I signed. It was going to be hard to work my way up the depth chart. The odds were against me in every way. Dad didn't tell me a lot about what was going on. I think it was to keep from getting my hopes up. I kept in shape after the season because I figured I was going to be playing somewhere.

(Photo by Beverly McHale)

Coach Mark McHale, left, reminisces with Brett Favre in the Green Bay quarterback's home in Mississippi in the room that contains memorabilia from his career.

Dad never made it out to be more or less than it was. He didn't bust my bubble. He never told me he thought it wasn't going to happen. He didn't build it up too much, either. He just let it happen.

I thought about it all the time. All the time, wondering what it would be like to play college football, about what team I'd play for. I felt like if I could just get the chance — that's all. If I could just get the chance I could show them what I could do. My problem was getting that chance and where would it be.

Chapter 6

The board and the official visit

Back in the meeting room our staff went over every name on the board, position by position. I looked up at the board and there was:

Brett Favre, Hancock North Central HS, 6-2, 185, 5.0 40-yard dash.

We had 13 quarterbacks listed and we planned to sign two. Brett's name was the last one. I don't believe I'd ever seen a kid listed that low get signed. The signing date was the first week of February. We were in late December. Brett's odds still were long. We already had gone from 23 quarterbacks to 13, though, so he still had a chance.

When his name came up in our discussion, I began my sales pitch. I told Coach Carmody that Brett was the best quarterback I'd ever seen. I told him about the tremendous arm and toughness. "Tough" was a key quality for Coach Carmody because the next question he asked me was, "Can he play defense." I told him Brett would start at free safety by the time he was a sophomore.

I was busy recruiting other players, too, but I made it a point to keep in touch with Brett to tell him to hang in there. With each call or visit, Irvin emphasized he was afraid of losing a scholarship to Delta State. I understood Irvin's apprehension. I tried my best to reassure him.

With each recruiting meeting, more players came off the board. In one weekend, we took five quarterbacks off the board. One committed to Alabama, another to LSU and a couple didn't make a high enough ACT score. The list was beginning to quickly dwindle. Brett's name was moving up the board, giving me more time to talk about him. Coach Carmody continually asked me if Brett could play other positions. He didn't want to waste a scholarship on a player who couldn't play quarterback and who didn't have the ability to play somewhere else on the field. I told Coach Carmody that Brett had the body frame and was tough enough to play free safety, linebacker or even tight end. I was really standing on the table for him and I finally

41

got approval to invite Brett and his parents for an official visit.

I was eager to tell Irvin and Brett. When coaches recruit, they get in a routine, visiting the same schools at the same times week after week, thanks to class schedules, geographical locations, basketball practices, free periods and such. For some reason, I always met with Irvin at 10 to 4, just as I did this time. Irvin and Brett were ecstatic with the news and we set up the official visit for the last weekend before the National Signing date. That would allow us leeway to offer Brett a scholarship if we lost other recruits we wanted. Coaches have to keep some recruits warm, just in case they don't get everyone they expect to sign.

The Favres expected the best outcome, but I told them again to be patient. I wasn't 100 percent sure Brett would be offered a scholarship. Because of what I heard in our recruiting meetings, though, I knew he had a chance. We ironed out the details on what to expect during the official visit. They would come up Friday evening and stay until Sunday morning. Our players would show Brett around town so he could get a feel for the social life. This stressful ordeal was fixing to get even more harrowing, but at least we had the other foot in the door.

After all the waiting and anticipation, the time had come for Brett to make his only official visit to a Division I campus. Brett was the only recruit I had in during this final weekend. All of the other players on my list had visited and were offered scholarships. I met Irvin, Bonita and Brett, got them registered at the hotel and took them to dinner at the Wagon Wheel restaurant. Afterwards, some of our players took Brett out for a night on the town while I talked with his parents about Brett's chances of being offered a scholarship. I told them it was in Coach Carmody's hands and that a lot depended on the other recruits we had in this weekend.

Brett was one of the last recruits scheduled to visit with Coach Carmody, so by the time Brett got to his office we probably would have a good idea of which recruits had accepted scholarships.

The next morning, I met the Favres for breakfast and asked Brett if he had a good time the night before.

"I had a great time, coach," Brett said. "We went out to a couple of nightspots and I really liked the guys I met. I met a lot of the football team at those places. Some of them are crazy!"

We drove over to the field house at the stadium; the entire coaching staff, some professors and our academic advisors were there. Coach Carmody greeted all the prospects and their families, introduced our staff and told the players which position coach they would meet. As

Coach Carmody introduced Jack White, I couldn't help but watch all of the Favres give him a hard look. They knew Jack was the person who evaluated Brett on tape. Brett's eyes got big as he sized up Jack and he wiggled in his chair.

We showed the players and their families a highlight film from our previous season. The film featured a lot of plays from our option offense, and Irvin and Brett were concerned about that. Our academic advisor addressed the players before the recruits were escorted by our "Golden Girls" hostesses to the buildings that housed their academic programs. Brett wasn't sure what his major would be, so he met with a representative who informed him and his parents of the various degrees he could pursue. Irvin and Bonita knew plenty about the academic programs, but Brett had one thing on his mind — football. He figured the academic side would take care of itself after he got into school.

We had lunch and got Brett back for his meeting with Jack White. They talked about the kind of offense Jack planned to implement and Brett was pleased to hear Jack mention more drop-back passing and play-action passing off the I-formation. There would be some option, but not to the extent we had run in the past. Jack told Brett he could tell by watching tapes that he had some talent throwing the ball. Brett bypassed the small talk and asked if he would receive a scholarship.

"It depends on what happens to the recruits we're looking at," Jack candidly said. "We've received one commitment from a quarterback already and we're waiting on two others. Michael Jackson is one of the others we're waiting on. It's between LSU and us."

Jackson was from Kentwood, La., and was the most valuable player of the state all-star game. He was a high-profile player and would have been a great catch for any program. Brett left Jack's office not knowing much more than when he went in. I asked Brett how his meeting with Jack went.

"I really like Coach White and I know I can play for him," Brett said. "I was excited about the passing game he covered with me and I think I would fit into this offense really well. I told him that I could play for him and I could play for him really soon."

Brett was not one to lack confidence. Irvin and Bonita listened intently as Brett talked about his meeting with Jack. Of course, they wanted to know if Jack had said anything about a scholarship. That patience that I had asked from them so often was starting to wear thin.

Brett went out with the Southern Miss players again and I took Irvin and Bonita out to dinner. They wanted to visit with some people they knew in Hattiesburg and we got together again for breakfast Sunday morning before their 10 o'clock meeting with Coach Carmody. After breakfast we sat in the lobby of the field house and Irvin and I looked at the pictures on the walls. Time seemed to take forever. Ten o'clock became 10:30, then 11. Coach Carmody was backed up in his meetings and it wasn't until 1 p.m. that Brett finally got to go in. I know Irvin and Bonita were irritated by the lengthy wait. They realized that they were the last family to meet with Coach Carmody. That means that Brett was the last recruit on the last weekend to meet with the head coach.

Some head coaches like for the assistant recruiting the player to sit in on the meeting with the family. Coach Carmody wasn't one of them. I had no idea what they were talking about. The Favres were in Coach Carmody's office half as long as the other recruits. When they came out, all three of them looked depressed. As I walked the Favres to their car, we talked about the meeting. Coach Carmody hadn't offered a scholarship. He told them it was a wait-and-see deal and that many recruits hadn't made decisions. A few might not even decide until National Signing Day. That news made for a long drive back to Kiln.

(University of Southern Mississippi photo)

Brett Favre was the last recruit to meet with Coach Jim Carmody on his official visit to Southern Mississippi. Favre and his parents weren't overly encouraged about the chances for a scholarship offer coming from the Golden Eagles after the meeting.

Our staff met immediately after the recruits left. We discussed how the weekend went and figured out who had committed that we thought we still had a chance to sign. We reviewed every name on the board in detail. When Coach Carmody got to Brett's name, he asked Jack how their meeting went and what he thought of him. Jack was very up front with his reply.

"The boy didn't lack any confidence, that's for sure," Jack said. "I liked him, but I like the other quarterbacks on the board ahead of him better from what I've seen on tape."

We continued discussing the other players on the board and things were coming to a head in a hurry. We had room for five more commitments to complete our signing class. In our meeting, it appeared one of the other quarterbacks was going to commit that night. All of us were on the phone all evening trying to get a feel for what would happen. We met again Monday morning.

We were having a tough time with the last five slots. I had landed four commitments from players in my area and was very excited that Chris Ryals was one of them. When we went through the board again, I learned we received a commitment from another quarterback. I got a really low feeling. I hated the idea of telling the Favres that it didn't work out. I was really hoping to get Brett a scholarship because I thought he deserved one. I also had become close to the Favre family, especially given the length of the recruiting process with Brett. Things didn't look good at all.

The entire staff was scrambling around all day, popping in and out of Coach Carmody's office to update him on the latest news. At 10:30 a.m., Coach Carmody stopped me in the hall and asked if Brett was still available. Suddenly, there was hope, however slim. I told him Brett was still available. Coach Carmody asked about Brett because we had lost a couple of linebackers we had badly wanted. We returned to the meeting room to go over the names another

 **Fact 4 Favre**

Brett Favre passed for 300-plus yards four times and 200-plus 11 times during his career at Southern Miss topped by a 345-yard performance against Memphis in 1989.

time. We had one more defensive player we were waiting on and he would complete our class. We left the meeting with that final spot up in the air. Later that day, Coach Carmody stopped me in the hall again.

"Mark, we lost the linebacker from Atlanta we talked about and I want you to call Brett Favre and tell him we have a scholarship for him," Coach Carmody said. "I'm going to fill out that defensive slot with him. We'll take him as a free safety."

I remember looking at my watch. I'll be darned if it wasn't 10 to 4! I rushed to the phone to tell the Favres the great news. Irvin answered the phone and I didn't tell him anything about the scholarship. I asked to speak to Brett, but he wasn't there. He was at a family member's house babysitting.

"I'll get him over here to the house right away," Irvin said.

I called back a short while later and Brett answered.

"Hey Coach McHale," Brett said nervously. "How's it going?"

I told him it was going really well and asked him if he was interested in a full scholarship to Southern Miss.

"Hell yeah I'm still interested," Brett said, enthusiastically.

I reminded Brett that he told me he could play for USM. I asked him if we gave him a scholarship would he disappoint me.

"You won't be sorry Coach McHale," Brett blurted.

That's when I told him he had a full scholarship to Southern Miss. Brett hollered to his family, "I got the scholarship! I got the scholarship!"

Brett got back on the phone and said, "You better believe I'll commit to you. Coach, I can't thank you enough for everything. Do you want to speak to Dad?"

Of course I did. Brett put him on the phone and it sounded like the whole family was hooting and hollering. Irvin was fired up.

"Coach McHale you won't be sorry," Irvin said. "Brett can play for you!"

I was really excited for the Favre family, for myself and for our football program. I just had a good feeling about the whole thing.

"You did not choose Me, but I chose you." – John 15:16.

BRETT'S VIEW

As late as the last couple of days before I was offered a scholarship Dad was telling me I'd probably have to go to a junior college or to a smaller school, so my thoughts were there. I thought I'd go to Pearl River Junior College or to Delta State or to one of those smaller schools. I wasn't aware at all how the change in offensive coordinators would impact anything.

I didn't know a lot about recruiting. I knew the guys from Pascagoula, Moss Point, Gulfport and Biloxi were getting all the attention. I picked up the papers and saw that, but I never had any interaction with any of those guys to talk about recruiting or anything like that. I was aware that they were being recruited and I was jealous and envied them.

I just wanted to play. I thought maybe I'd play safety, although I thought I'd be better at quarterback, and I wasn't stupid. I wanted to play college football at whatever position. I'd punt, play receiver, whatever, I just wanted a chance to play. I just wanted to get my foot in the door and I thought one way to do that was on defense because there was more tape of me tackling and intercepting and things like that.

When I was invited to visit Southern Miss, I thought that was great. I knew it didn't guarantee anything and Dad was good about that. He told me the invitation to visit was good, but he didn't get my hopes

46

Brett Favre is just another guy away from the football field. He relaxes at home by working around the house, in particular in his yard.

up. I thought Southern Miss still had a lot of interest and I had a lot of interest in them because I had no other official visits from any other teams. I thought it was good that the door still was open, even though I didn't think it really was. In my mind, it wasn't a done deal. Where it went from the visit I wasn't sure. Some of the other players I'd talked to, Chris Ryals and some of those guys who Southern Miss was recruiting, they were in the process of narrowing down where they wanted to go. With me there was no narrowing it down. I was more nervous than most guys because of that.

Chris was an All-American and all that. Michael Jackson and guys like that who Southern Miss was recruiting had a track record that everyone knew about. Guys asked me who I played for, what I did, how many yards I threw for. Guys get to talking like that, about all that stuff. I was thinking I didn't have a whole lot to show. It was starting to hit me that I was making this official visit. I had been a big shot at Hancock. I was excited about going, but I was the lowest man on the totem pole and I was well aware of that.

I had no official visits other than to Southern Miss. Nowhere. When we pulled into the parking lot at Southern Miss and I got out of the van, that probably was my first dose of big-time college football. This wasn't Hancock County anymore. Even at that, it was still in my mind that I was a long way from receiving a scholarship, even though I was on campus and right by the stadium.

I remember looking at the stadium and, I've played at a lot of stadiums since, but it was still kind of big-time for me then. That's never changed. I've come a long way since then, but I'm still aware I wasn't at Hancock anymore, I wasn't the big man on campus and I didn't know if I ever would be again. Reality was setting in. Nobody knew me and nobody really cared. Where it was going from there was a toss-up. A lot of those guys who were visiting, they probably were promised stuff by various schools. They probably were looking for a lot more than I was looking for. They had gotten a lot more attention.

It became evident when I got there that there were guys being treated differently. There were guys getting catered to a lot more than I was. There was a point on that official weekend visit where we walked out on to the football field. I didn't doubt I could play there. I knew just how close I was, but how far away I was, too. You have to crawl before you can walk and I was crawling. I had envisioned myself playing on that field.

At that time, I had envisioned myself playing pro ball. It was hitting me that I needed to get my priorities in line. I started thinking it would be amazing if I could just make the traveling squad. It's amazing the steps I saw myself taking. Some of the other guys weren't talking traveling squad. Shoot, if they didn't play they were going to be disappointed. Where I was, I just wanted to get signed. I'd just started getting my first taste of it.

When we watched the highlight tape, it didn't strike me that this wasn't my kind of offense, the option. I was thinking I could do this, but I looked around the room and thought I can't run the option like Michael Jackson, not that I'd ever seen him play, but just gauging myself against the other people I was seeing and had heard about and what I was seeing on the film. I was actually thinking my odds were getting worse. Then I was thinking I might make the team but would I play?

When I met Coach White, I was intimidated because I wasn't real savvy I guess in the Xs and Os department. I never was really taught that. Dad taught me differently. We did drills. We hit the sleds. That was more of what I could talk shop about. It wasn't about the curl and the flat read or how you read this or that. We never did the three-step, five-step and seven-step drops. It was double reverse roll.

Coach White talked a little football. I'm sure that's what every coach kind of has to do. I'm sure he wanted to kind of gauge where I was from a knowledge standpoint. I was way behind. Way behind. Coach White probably looked at the paperwork and saw I had thrown for eight touchdowns and was more of an option guy. I wanted him to get to know me more from a physical standpoint. I had all the tools. I mean I had the size, decent speed. All he had to do was take me out and watch me throw three or four passes and he'd know I had the arm, but he wanted to find out more and I didn't know if I could give him what he wanted to hear. I couldn't talk shop with him.

I knew I had the size. I was 6-foot, 180 (pounds), maybe 185, something like that. I was strong. I worked out a lot. I was running and doing all that stuff. I think from a physical standpoint I was going to be fine. I wished I was a little taller, but at 17 you do that no matter how big you are. I never felt from a physical standpoint, though, that I lacked anything. That part was in place. That part could hold its own.

During my visit, I was thinking football. Academics didn't mean anything to me. Getting a scholarship, my books and tuition would be paid for. Every guy there probably had aspirations of playing pro ball, but you had to think as most parents were thinking — this is a free education. That would save my family a ton of money, but my only thoughts were that I had to get a scholarship to play football.

Academically, I was happy. I probably could have been better, but I worked a lot harder in sports than I did in school, where a lot of guys would go to college and were just glad sports was paying for their college. I went to class just to keep myself eligible, thinking I would play pro football and that would pay all the bills and all that stuff. That was such a long shot, but that's the way I thought.

Even with all of that, from day one I think I thought I was going to make my living playing pro football. I always thought that way. I'm sure a lot of kids think that way and I'm no different than anyone else. I'm glad I finally realized how great the odds were. There are a lot of great players who have come through college who never even got a chance to show what they could do. How it all fell into place for me is amazing because it wasn't like they just opened the doors for me wherever I went. Being naive and unaware of a lot of things probably was best for me. It probably was best that people weren't opening doors and stuff because I worked harder to overcome a lot higher odds than a lot of other people.

I was excited about the visit, which to me was great, but I knew that the odds were against me. When I left the meeting with the head coach, it was the same as when I went into that meeting. I knew whether it was 15 minutes or an hour and 15 minutes the odds still were against me getting a scholarship. Again, that was the attention the other guys were getting compared to what I was getting. I didn't have to be a rocket scientist to figure out that they weren't promising me anything.

Mom and Dad knew it didn't look good and they were disappointed. I was just happy to be there. Whatever happened happened, but they were more aware of what was going on than I was. I think Dad tried to keep most of the anxiety from me and I commend him for that.

When Coach McHale called me to tell me I had a scholarship I was at my Aunt Lane's house sort of babysitting her two kids. I was shocked when he told me because I thought all the colleges pretty much had recruiting wrapped up. It was like a gift on Christmas that I wasn't expecting. My hopes weren't up and I figured I'd just go ahead and sign with a program like Delta State. I remember thinking it was too good to be true. It was great. It was probably as big, if not bigger, than the (NFL) Draft.

I wouldn't change it. I wouldn't have it any other way because for a guy who is highly recruited, there are bigger expectations. There are more decisions to be made on where to go, was this the right decision, things like that. I didn't have to worry about that. In the draft, there probably are more Top-10 picks who are busts than there are late-round picks who succeed and that was no different than recruiting for me.

No one expected anything of me so I didn't have to live up to anything. Not knowing a lot about the process made it much easier for me. I didn't have to worry about having picked the wrong school. If I got the chance, I wanted to make the most of it. If it failed — and I didn't expect it to fail — then it happened. I didn't have to live up to certain expectations the way a lot of guys did. I was well aware that I might be recruited as a safety. I just wanted to go up there as a football player. That was fine with me. I just wanted to play.

When the signing was done, we really didn't do anything special. I was glad it was done. There was a sigh of relief more than anything. I might have walked down the hall of my school with my chest a little poked out, but some people kind of looked at me with jealousy. They thought the only reason I got any recognition was because my dad was the coach, which to a certain extent was true. I never had much interaction with any of those classmates, teammates or anything like that. I had a one-track mind and was determined to succeed, even though the odds were against me. I felt proud of what I had accomplished, but I always felt like I was looking over my shoulder because people would like to stab me in the back. I couldn't wait to get out and pursue a college career. It was one big step in the direction I wanted to go.

Chapter **7**

Number 4

With National Signing Day over, Coach Carmody decided to reward the staff with a trip to Mardi Gras on New Orleans' famous Fat Tuesday. I was excited about the trip. I'd heard about Mardi Gras and had seen a little bit of it on TV. The team bus took our staff on the two-hour trip to New Orleans. We parked at the Superdome and were to meet there at midnight to return to Hattiesburg.

Jim Tompkins, our defensive line coach, and I walked to the French Quarter and Jim asked if I wanted to go down to Bourbon Street for breakfast. We found an oyster bar and ate a mountain of raw oysters we washed down with tomato juice. When we went out on the sidewalk, it was wall-to-wall people. I'd never seen anything like it. There were people running around in all kinds of costumes, some of them half-naked. Some of the things I saw I can't even begin to describe. It was so crowded all you could do was go along with the flow. I lost Jim in the crowd and didn't see him again until midnight.

I walked all over town and wound up at a parade site where I was bombarded with beads. It was starting to get dark and I headed up Bourbon Street again when I felt a tap on my shoulder.

"What are you doing, boy," a voice asked me.

I turned around and saw a man with his face all painted. It took me a few seconds to realize it was Gerald Goodman, our wide receivers coach. Gerald told me Coach Carmody had a friend who owned a restaurant on Bourbon Street and we needed to go there for dinner. We found the restaurant but not the rest of our party, so Gerald and I hung out until it was time to go back to the Superdome. When we got back to the Superdome, everyone was there but there was no bus. Coach Carmody and I went to look for the bus while everyone else waited. I had no idea where I was, let alone where the bus might be, but we split up to check the side streets.

I was tired, so I stopped at the corner of St. Louis and Bourbon and leaned against a streetlight. I was there a few minutes when behind me

I heard the loudest horn I'd ever heard. I jumped and turned around to see our bus, with our driver Tom Curtis laughing his butt off. Tom explained that the security people at the Superdome wouldn't let him stay there, so he drove around until he got jammed in this spot.

We made our way back to the Superdome and I soaked in the praise for singlehandedly, without regard for my own life, heroically finding the bus and bringing it back. Tom let me bask in the glory for a while before offering his version of the bus rescue story, which differed greatly from my tale.

When we got back to campus we began an off-season workout program that continued right up to spring practice. We invited our recruits in for the spring game at the end of April, and Irvin and Brett were thrilled to be there. Brett got a good look at our team during the spring game and, after evaluating our offense, told me he thought he could play quarterback for us next year. There was that healthy dose of self-confidence coming through again. Brett never doubted himself. I knew, though, he had a long way to go to make the transition from high school to college.

 **Fact 4 Favre**

Brett Favre's longest touchdown pass at Southern Mississippi covered 80 yards to Ron Braham against Texas A&M in 1989.

Brett met Chris Ryals at the spring game. They hit it off pretty well and stayed in touch through the summer. They decided they wanted to be roommates when they reported for summer camp. Brett always liked hanging out with the offensive linemen.

When you're a football coach, time flies. Our spring game was over and we hit the road for spring recruiting. I stopped by Hancock North to visit Irvin and Brett. Irvin had been selected to coach in the Mississippi High School All-Star Game in Jackson and Brett had played baseball all summer. Brett was going to play in the all-star game, but was on the roster as a strong safety. I was excited for Brett, yet confused at the same time. Here was a high school coach on staff and his son wasn't going to play quarterback. That kind of blew my mind, but I didn't make a big deal out of it.

I wasn't going to see Irvin or Brett again before the report to campus in August so I wanted to spend some quality time with both of them. We talked about the long and stressful recruiting process we had gone through and about how happy we all were with the way it turned out. I stressed to Brett the importance of weightlifting. Not only would it improve his athletic ability, it would be a great tool in prevention of injuries. I told Brett he was going to be taking some hits from players who were a lot bigger, faster and stronger than he saw in high school and his joints needed to be as strong as they could be. Irvin guaranteed me Brett would hit the weights.

"Coach McHale, I'll make sure he stays on a good weight program throughout the summer," Irvin said. "Brett will report to you in great shape."

We talked about the reporting date and the schedule for two-a-day practices. Brett asked me if he could request Chris Ryals as his roommate. He said he and Chris had been calling one another since they met and that they wanted to room together. I knew Coach Carmody liked players to room with guys from a like position. He felt they would study together and share their football knowledge with one another. I told Brett I would mention it, but couldn't guarantee anything. Most quarterbacks like to room with other quarterbacks, not 6-foot-7, 300-pound linemen. Brett, though, wasn't just any quarterback.

I finished my May recruiting and looked forward to a vacation in June. I got a call from Bugs Moffett, who lived in Winchester, Va. Bugs remembered the promise I made of a vacation in New Orleans and was going to hold me to it. He already had planned to fly into Hattiesburg and I was all for it. I told him I was going to introduce him to this stuff they called "gumbo" and that he'd never tasted anything like it. I promised to take him to Bourbon Street and to bayou country.

I looked forward to seeing Bugs. It had been a long year, changing jobs, going right into football season and recruiting so much. Recruiting Brett was stressful because it went right down to the wire and all of that added to my needing some rest and relaxation. We had a great time in New Orleans, even if it didn't last long enough. I came back refreshed and dove right into football camp, where some very promising players from my area participated.

July melted into August and our freshmen were to report Aug. 12. Our staff met to prepare room assignments. I couldn't work things out for Brett and Chris to room together. Brett was assigned to room with a linebacker from Slidell, La. I think Coach Carmody thought Brett would be a linebacker before the end of summer camp.

Sometimes we take for granted the little things that go into team chemistry. Roommates, room location, jersey numbers and such things are important to young men. When our players reported, I met the ones I had signed and helped them get settled in. I spent a lot of time with their parents, reassuring them their sons would be OK. This was the first time away from home for most of these kids. We had a team meeting that night and the freshmen had a chance to meet one another.

The first freshman meeting is quite an experience. They were given special attention during recruiting and undoubtedly felt like they were at the high point of their young lives. They had been hometown heroes and most had been courted by several universities. They were with their proud parents who had bragged on them their entire lives and met their needs.

Now it was time to sever the umbilical cord. Who was going to wake them up the next morning? Who was going to cook their favorite breakfast? For the first time it was hitting these guys that they were alone in a room filled with some of the better athletes throughout the country. They had to wonder if they would live up to the expectations placed on them by their families and themselves. How would they fare against better competition, competing for a position with 20-year-old men who had more experience, more weight training and who were tested on the playing field against the likes of Florida State and Alabama of the college football world.

 **Fact 4 Favre**

Brett Favre's career high for completions at Southern Miss came against East Carolina in 1989 when he connected on 26 of 35 passes for 286 yards.

Coach Carmody welcomed the freshmen and covered his expectations for them before turning the meeting over to the administrative staff who went over the next day's agenda. There was a lot to cover. Much was to be done before any of them put on a uniform. The next day the freshmen would need to finalize their academic schedules, meet their advisors, take a physical, participate in physical tests directed by the coaching staff and get fitted for equipment.

No longer were they the big-name star, but for a while were relegated to a mere letter, the first of their last names. Those with names beginning with A through G were to visit their academic advisors; H through M were to get physicals; N through Z were to receive their equipment. All of them were to report to breakfast at 6 a.m. and head to their assigned stations one hour later.

The equipment station was the most important to Brett. He was intent on receiving his high school jersey number — 10. Brett figured since no one wore No. 10 last season it would be available to him. To increase his chances of getting No. 10, he planned to show up early.

(Photo by Beverly McHale)

Brett Favre requested his high school No. 10 when he arrived at Southern Mississippi, but quickly discovered it had been retired in honor of former Golden Eagles' star quarterback Reggie Collier. Favre was given No. 4, which the school retired in his honor in 1993.

The A through G group was to report to the equipment cage at 4 p.m. Brett showed up 10 minutes early — at 10 to 4.

David Bounds was the equipment manager and he made it a point to break the freshmen in to his operating procedures right off the bat. His demeanor left no doubt he would not give special treatment to anyone. All-American or walk-on, they all received the same treatment from David. When David opened the cage, Brett was first in line.

"We'll start by assigning you a jersey number so we can mark all your equipment," David said. "What position are you?"

Brett forcefully said, "I'm a quarterback and I want my high school number, 10."

David paused, then enlightened Brett that No. 10 wasn't available.

"That number has just been retired. It belonged to Reggie Collier and he was drafted into the NFL, so we retired it this year," David said. "What other number do you want?"

Brett was sure he was going to get No. 10. For players, their number is their identity. In high school, he wore it everywhere. It was how he was recognized for all he had accomplished. All his friends back home

55

would recognize him by that number. It's the number they would look for when they watched the games on TV. To be denied access to that particular number was severing of that identity.

Brett was heartbroken, but had to think quickly. He liked Roger Staubach and Terry Bradshaw, so he asked for No. 12.

"No," David said. "Sorry. That number has already been taken."

"Give me No. 11, then," Brett said.

"That one is taken, too," David said.

"What number can I have, then," Brett asked, getting frustrated.

"I've got one number left," David said. "It's number 4. Take it or leave it."

Brett wasn't about to leave it, so he took No. 4. He didn't like it much and he didn't identify with it at all. He was just going to have to develop an identity for that number as he made the transition from 10 to 4.

With the prerequisites out of the way, I visited the dorms that night to see how the guys I signed were doing. I got to Brett's room and he didn't look happy. I asked if he was all right and he told me it wasn't anything he couldn't handle. He said he was disappointed about the jersey number and he didn't care for his roommate. I told Brett I was sorry about the jersey number and that even though I couldn't get him in a room with Chris Ryals I did get Chris in the room next to him. Doors connected Brett's and Chris' rooms because they shared a bathroom. I knew Brett would get to see a lot of Chris and I told him not to get distracted and to concentrate on playing quarterback at Southern Miss.

"All right, coach," Brett said. "I won't let you down."

Numerous things cause players to get homesick and as a coach you have to be alert to the signs. I didn't want Brett to get homesick and leave, so I kept a close eye on him throughout summer camp.

We had the freshmen in a few days before the varsity so we could evaluate them, select those we thought could play early and introduce them to our system. Getting the players familiar with the system would help keep them from being intimidated by the varsity players. We had six practices with the freshmen. The offense worked out in the morning and the defense in the afternoon. The freshmen practice both an offensive and a defensive position. The defensive staff observed the players in the morning and the offense got a look in the afternoon. This helped ensure that the players were in the right positions to help our football team. We met as a staff after each session to discuss the

56

(Favre family photo)

The Favre family as well as numerous cousins, aunts, and uncles were fixtures at Southern Mississippi football games during Brett's career.

progress of each player.

If we felt we had a player who had to play a certain position and it wasn't the position he wanted to play, we would meet with him after the sixth practice session and explain to him how he could best help our football team. We then placed the player in the position where we needed him when our full-team practice began. Sometimes a freshman didn't like the move, but he had to adjust.

The day before the varsity was to report, we had our final personnel meeting about the freshmen. We went through the quarterback position and got to Brett's name. Coach Carmody asked Jack what he thought of Brett as a quarterback. Jack didn't go overboard in his praise and Coach Carmody suggested we move Brett to linebacker.

"No, let's not do that just yet," Jack said. "Let me see some more of him at quarterback and see how he does when the varsity comes in."

Brett wasn't getting a lot of repetitions when he went through the pass skeleton part of practice. Pass skeleton has the quarterbacks throwing to the backs and receivers against linebackers and the secondary. With just three practices dedicated to offense and several quarterbacks in the rotation, it was difficult to get a feel for the quarterbacks that early. I'm sure, though, Jack saw the velocity Brett put on the football. If he didn't like Brett as a quarterback, he would have let Coach Carmody move him at that time. The defensive staff didn't have strong feelings about moving Brett, either, so he stayed at quarterback.

Jack wasn't really thinking Brett could help us as a freshman, although he thought Brett could help in the future. He was more concerned with polishing up Alrick Young and Simmie Carter, each of whom had been introduced to the system in spring practice. Both were very good athletes. Getting a true evaluation on all seven quarterbacks was a challenge. Jack's main concern was to have two ready when we opened the season against Alabama.

> **"Trust in the Lord with all your heart, and do not rely on your own understanding; think about Him in all your ways, and He will guide you on the right paths." – Proverbs 3:5-6.**

BRETT'S VIEW

They had me playing both offense and defense my first week at Southern Miss. There weren't a lot of people throwing passes. I thought quarterback wasn't going to happen. I only got to throw passes when I was giving the defense a look.

I wanted jersey No. 10 and the equipment guy said I couldn't have it because it was Reggie Collier's. Before I could say much of anything I had No. 4. Today, you see more single digits than you did back then. I wasn't picky, but No. 4? That was like a punter or a receiver or something. But then again, I was thinking that's kind of how I fit in to this deal. It was like reality setting in.

I was a nobody where some freshmen were getting first dibs on numbers. I was last on the depth chart and I was last on the number I got because college is a heck of a lot different than the pros. There are 100 players and you don't know anybody. Nobody wears 101, so I said I'd take 4 and like it. It's worked out pretty well.

My first stages at Southern Miss I was competitive, but I was just trying to get on the field. I couldn't think of everybody else out there until I got out there, but I think that's part of being a true competitor.

You want to do it for everybody, not just your own job.

In our first meeting, I was nervous based on where I would fit in. Chris Ryals was all-everything. Michael Jackson was the player of the year in Louisiana. I didn't have any of that.

At practice with the rest of the freshmen before the varsity reported, I remember that we all didn't get the same amount of reps. Michael probably got the most because he fit what they were trying to do. I was an unknown. Most of the stuff we ran were options and most of the throwing were roll outs and things like that. All that stuff was new to me. Not the option, but the way we ran it. All the stuff I did in high school was misdirection and things like that. I had a lot to learn. They could tell me what to do, but I needed the reps to get it and I wasn't getting many reps.

When the varsity reported I felt like a fish out of water. How was I going to get noticed in this group?

I was glad to get to Southern Miss. At the end of my senior year of high school was the first time I'd ever had a real job. I worked in Diamondhead, a little community right there near the house. I was with the maintenance department, which meant you do whatever. I was 17 and going in at 6 in the morning. That was early.

(Favre family photo)

Brett Favre (4) and lineman Chris Ryals were two of Mark McHale's key recruits in his first season at Southern Mississippi. The two players quickly became friends after reporting for pre-season camp as freshmen.

We'd play baseball at night or we'd practice. We'd practice at Long Beach or at Harrison Central High School. I'd get off work, weed eating one day, cutting grass the next, raking or picking up trash the next. About 3:30 in the afternoon I'd get off and go play baseball and by 9 at night I was burned out. In there somewhere I'd always find time to work out, running the stadium or the roads, running hundreds at the football field.

Scott was in town and we'd go up there and just throw. I didn't do any five-step drops or have anybody run routes or anything. I'd tell Scott "just go down there 50 yards and I'll throw 20 balls to you." It was that type of stuff. I never worked on timing or anything like that.

That summer I was selected to play in the state all-star game as a

Brett Favre (4) signs an autograph for a young Southern Mississippi fan with a teammate during Media Day as a freshman.

safety. I wanted to play quarterback. I remember Kevin Joiner was the quarterback from Moss Point and the head coach was Billy Miller from Moss Point. Kevin signed with the University of Minnesota out of high school. He had thrown for 4,000 yards and 30 or 40 touchdowns, so I was intimidated before I even met the guy. I was disappointed but it was like when I went to Southern Miss. I just sucked it up and did whatever it took.

I watched the other quarterbacks in that all-star game and I felt I stacked up pretty good. I felt I could do some things nobody else could do. So I felt I had a chance to play quarterback in college. So when I got to Southern Miss I wanted to do things that made the coaches say, "Whoa! If we can harness this we've got something." When I had an opportunity I had to make the most of it.

Chapter 8

Elway! Elway!

The varsity reported Aug. 15 and we had a meeting with the entire squad after dinner. The room was full, with 100 players, the coaching staff and the support staff taking up nearly every inch. This can be intimidating to a freshman who has grown accustomed to plenty of individual attention from his position coach the last three days. The freshmen looked around and saw a room filled with players who were bigger and more mature. The older players eyeballed the freshmen as if they were stalking prey for the rest of two-a-day practices. Some whispered and pointed their fingers at some of the freshmen. This certainly wasn't going to ease the mind of any kid who was homesick.

This meeting was twice as long as the first one the freshmen had experienced. Every rule was covered in great detail, along with every phase of the football program. The freshmen then were asked to introduce themselves by standing, giving their name, position and where they were from. All obviously were nervous when their turns came.

The varsity reported at 6 a.m. the next morning for strenuous physical tests to make sure they were in shape. The freshmen were there to observe the conditioning tests. That afternoon, the news media came in to interview the varsity players and the new recruits. Brett didn't get much attention that day. He wasn't highly publicized coming out of high school. His family and some relatives came up for press day and to see Brett.

We had a staff meeting that afternoon to go over our personnel and to make some moves with the freshmen. We had seven quarterbacks listed. Ailrick Young was at the top of the depth chart, with Simmie Carter a close second. David Forbes was third, followed by highly touted Michael Jackson. Brett was at the very bottom, the seventh quarterback heading into pre-season camp.

Young and Carter got a lot of reps to get ready for Alabama. Forbes got some work, too, and Jackson received a few reps to see how he would respond when going against the varsity. Brett had gotten all the reps he was going to get. There were just too many quarterbacks, so Jack sent Brett down to work with the scout team. The scout team simulates the opponent. Brett ran plays from cards that were shown to him between plays.

After each practice we met as a staff to talk about our personnel and progress. After a few days, the defensive staff was bragging on Brett and how he was tearing up the defense with his throwing arm. Brett was getting noticed, which meant the head coach was taking notice, too. Because Jack was working with four other quarterbacks, he had no idea what Brett was doing.

Our camp featured three major scrimmages before game week. The scrimmages were designed to evaluate personnel and to develop who would be starters, reserves and who would make the travel squad. The first-team units went against the second-team squads for the most part. Once in a while we would have the first-team offense go against the first-team defense. After a designated number of plays, we let the third-team unit and those below scrimmage against one another. Once in a while we let the first team go against the third team to let the third teamers get a taste of what it was like to go against the type of talent it took to start.

Brett had to alternate with two other quarterbacks on the third team. It was difficult for those guys because they didn't get the reps to run our offense. They knew more about running an opponent's offense than they did ours. Their timing with the receivers wasn't there and their ball handling wasn't very polished.

We had gone through two major scrimmages and Brett was yet to do anything outstanding. Heading to our third scrimmage, two quarterbacks were out with injuries. We let Young and Carter work with the first and second units. When it came time for the third teamers to scrimmage, Brett got a lot of action. The offensive line wasn't very polished, so Brett didn't get much protection. Brett did manage to scramble and make some good throws for completions. He was looking pretty good.

We took a break before ending our last phase of the scrimmage. Coach Carmody announced that the first team was going against the third team, sparking all kinds of taunting noises from the varsity to intimidate the freshmen. This was kind of an initiation ritual for the freshmen. The varsity players were singling out who they were going to get. The energy level had risen to a high on a hot Saturday afternoon despite two hours of work.

What happened next was one of the most amazing feats I'd ever witnessed. Brett was the only healthy quarterback, so it was his job to lead the third team. These guys could hardly remember what to do on any given play without reading a card because they had not had many reps with our offense. The third team offense started from its own 35-yard line. The offensive coaches got in the huddle to call a play and help them with their assignments. Jack gave Brett the first play to call. It was a basic running play. Brett called the signals and handed off to a reluctant running back who got crushed in the backfield by a bunch of fired up defensive players.

The starters were taunting and yelling and those poor freshmen were scared to death. They came back to the huddle looking at each other with very little confidence. I overheard Brett talking to Jack while the offense was huddling.

"Let me throw the ball, coach," Brett pleaded.

Jack told Brett to settle down and gave him a three-step drop passing play he could get off without getting creamed. Brett stepped into the huddle and told the line to keep the defense off him so he could complete a pass. Brett gave the play, the snap count and broke the huddle. He talked to the

Fact 4 Favre

Brett Favre's year-by-year passing totals at Southern Mississippi

Freshman: 79-194, 1,264 yards 15 touchdowns, 13 interceptions

Sophomore: 178-319, 2,271 yards, 16 touchdowns, 5 interceptions

Junior: 206-381, 2,588 yards, 14 touchdowns, 10 interceptions

Senior: 150-275, 1,572 yards, 7 touchdowns, 6 interceptions

receivers on the way to the line of scrimmage. Brett had a take-control air about him from the beginning.

Brett stepped under center and took the snap. In a flash one of the defensive linemen broke through the line and came up the middle to try for a sack, but Brett shook him off and scrambled to his right. Brett was running as hard as he could and pointing to where he wanted the receiver to run the pattern. Several defenders gained on Brett but he drew back his arm and launched a rocket. We all could hear the ball hit the receivers shoulder pads. It was a 15-yard completion.

You could see the eyes of the offensive players light up as they felt pride in getting a first down against the first-team defense. Jack was grinning from ear to ear as he gave Brett another pass play. This time Jack got greedy and called a five-step drop, meaning the line would have to hold the defense out even longer this time. Brett again confidently called the play in the huddle, took the snap and dropped back 7 yards. The rush was on him again and he calmly sidestepped the defender and fired another bullet that hit the receiver right on the money for a 20-yard gain.

We ran the ball the next two plays and didn't gain an inch. The defense was regaining its confidence and was taunting again. Jack called another pass play and Brett scrambled before throwing the ball out of bounds. Coach Carmody called for the second team to go in for the third team. There were plenty of third- and fourth-team players to alternate in and out, but Brett stayed in. The next drive began on the offense's 40. Brett threw the ball on almost every down and was tearing the defense apart. We could see the rest of our team getting excited by what they were seeing from Brett.

On the next play, Brett completed a 20-yard pass that made a cracking sound as the receiver caught it. John Baylor, who was a starting defensive end, started chanting, "Elway!

(Doug Collier/Getty Images)

Brett Favre drew comparisons to NFL Hall of Famer John Elway during one of his first scrimmages at Southern Mississippi. Teammates shouted, "Elway, Elway" after Favre's pass zipped across the field into the hands of receivers. Here the two are talking before an NFL exhibition game in the late 1990s.

Elway!" in reference to the arm of All-Pro quarterback John Elway of the Denver Broncos. The rest of the defense picked up on it and continued the chant louder and louder.

I turned and looked at defensive end coach Gene Smith and he asked, "that's the Favre boy from Hancock isn't it Mark? Look how that boy gets our defensive players excited. I don't think I've ever seen anything like this before." I told Gene that Brett got me excited, too.

I glanced at Coach Carmody and I could see the wheels turning. He didn't say or do anything, but I could see it in his eyes. He knew we had something special.

Brett took the unit right down the field and ended the drive with a touchdown pass. He jumped up and down and signaled touchdown with his arms just like he did that night I saw him in high school. He was having the time of his life. It was contagious. The rest of the third-teamers were jumping up and down with excitement as if their team had scored. When Brett came to the sideline, the defensive starters were congratulating him. He had won their respect.

We had three more practices before starting the game plan for Alabama. Our final scrimmage was a mock simulating Alabama. The coaches moved the ball around the field to simulate all the situations that could happen in a game. We also involved our special teams to give them a realistic feel for field position.

Classes started that Monday, marking the end of two-a-day practices. At our staff meeting, Coach Carmody was talking about our quarterback situation. He told Jack not to worry about red-shirting Brett and that he would like to see him get some action in the first game.

"Coach, I don't know how he can be ready," Jack said. "He hasn't been through pass skeleton with us and he doesn't even know our plays."

I'll never forget what Coach Carmody said next.

"Anybody that gets my defense as excited as he does, I don't care if he knows the plays or not," he said. "Just see what you can do to get him some experience."

I was shocked! We were getting ready to play Alabama and we were talking about playing a freshman named Brett Favre. We weren't even going to offer him a scholarship seven months before and even when we did he came to camp a month earlier as the No. 7 quarterback. Now, we were preparing him to play against one of the most storied programs in the history of college football. I was feeling really good about signing this guy.

I went over to the dorm that night to see Brett. When I got to the room I could hear a lot of noise coming from inside. I knocked on the door and when it opened I saw Brett and Chris Ryals on the floor wrestling. They had three mattresses arranged on the floor and Brett had this big lineman in a headlock. The stereo was playing so loud they didn't hear me come in. I yelled, "what the heck is going on here boys!"

(University of Southern Mississippi photo)

Had Brett Favre been given adequate practice time from the first days of pre-season camp his freshman season, he may very well have been Southern Mississippi's starting quarterback in the season-opener.

"Hey, coach," Brett said. "What's up?"

I told them they were up if they didn't settle down. I told Chris he was going to hurt that little quarterback if he wasn't careful. Chris, sounding as innocent as he could, put the onus on Brett.

"Coach, this guy is crazy," Chris said. "I can't keep him off me. He jumps on me all the time."

I teased Chris that I'd get him a bouncer up there to keep watch and to protect him from this animal from Kiln.

"That's right, coach," Brett chimed in. "You tell baby Huey that he needs protection."

That really got to Chris and he started telling Brett how he was going to hurt him. They were just boys playing around. Still, it was unusual to see this 185-pound quarterback harassing this big offensive lineman.

I asked why the mattresses were on the floor and why there were three of them in a room made for two people.

"Coach, we can't stand that other guy so we all three moved in here and put him in the other room by himself," Brett said.

I told them Coach Carmody would be none too happy with that setup and that one of them was going to have to move next door and that they could decide among themselves who it would be. Then I told Brett I needed to talk to him in the hall. Brett came out and shut the door behind him. I fussed at Brett for messing with Chris, whose nickname was Purvis after his hometown. I told him he could hurt his arm and not be able to practice.

I then told Brett that he'd done a great job in our scrimmage. I encouraged him to study his playbook, pay attention in meetings and watch the other quarterbacks in skeleton. I told him he never could be sure when another quarterback might get hurt and that he needed to be ready to play. Brett listened intently.

"Coach McHale, I'll be ready," Brett said. "I just don't get any reps in practice. It's hard to get the offense down by just watching."

I told Brett he had climbed to No. 3 on the depth chart and that he'd be getting more reps. The first two quarterbacks had been through spring practice and knew the offense better. Brett was going to have to catch up by being a great student of the game. I told him to approach each practice as if he was going to be the starter. Brett's eyes lit up.

"OK, coach," Brett said. "I'll study really hard. You can count on me."

I poked my head in the room and kidded Chris again about the animal from Kiln. Then I told them to get the roommate situation figured out before they got in the doghouse. Chris turned red and I knew he was going to give Brett a tongue lashing.

I really didn't expect Brett to play against Alabama. I couldn't see how he could until he learned the offense. He hadn't had any reps and there was no way he could learn an offense in just four days. It would be hard for him to learn it all even if he took every rep by himself. I just wanted him to be ready in case opportunity presented itself down the road. It was obvious our head coach liked something about Brett or he wouldn't ask that Brett be given playing time in our first game.

> **"For God has not given us a spirit of fearfulness, but one of power, love and sound judgment." – 2 Timothy 1:7.**

BRETT'S VIEW

Once we started practicing, I didn't know what to expect. I figured the last guy on the depth chart got the least amount of reps and it seemed like the younger players were picked on more by the coaches. They would ask, "what's the play" and if you're standing back there looking around and didn't know what the play meant you'd get chewed on by the coaches. If your steps were a little off it was embarrassing. I was embarrassed to get called out, so as much as I wanted reps I was reluctant to jump in there because I didn't always know where to go.

It's tough because you have to take charge but you know you're not in charge. I was the last man on the totem pole, but when they tell you to get in there it's your only opportunity and you don't want to mess it up. I had to act like I knew what I was doing. I knew I had to crawl before I walked, but how could I convince them I was confident when I was shaking in my boots? I didn't get as many reps as the other guys. That wasn't fair, but it's the way it was.

In the meetings it was really tough — all the terminology and checks. I'd never heard of checks. All that stuff was new to me. I was so much further behind those other guys. Sure, the terminology is new to everyone but at least they knew the concept. To me, it all meant nothing. In high school, we just ran plays. A double reverse was a double reverse. This was all new to me.

My first scrimmage I was thinking "don't screw it up." But more importantly I was thinking, "set yourself apart from the other guys." That's hard to do. I had to make the other 10 guys believe I knew what I was doing and make them believe I could carry them where we wanted to go. All that was going through my mind, but they didn't care who I was. They were trying to set themselves apart and make a mark on the team, too.

Quarterback's a tough position. You're trying to lead not only yourself but the rest of the guys. I learn best from the reps. When the bullets start to fly you find out what people are made of. I had to act like I knew what I was doing and somehow make it work.

That third scrimmage, I was doing things but they weren't the way they were drawn up. As I walked off the field that day I knew what I had to do. It was a step in the right direction, but I knew I was still a long way from being where I wanted to be. I got a chance and had made the most of it. I had gotten noticed.

Off the field, I liked hanging with Chris Ryals and those linemen. It was just my kind of mentality. You know, old dirtbag tough, in-the-trenches-type of guys. Those prima donna guys who can't be touched and all that stuff, that was never me. It was nothing for me to throw a block or two or make a tackle or do whatever the team needed me to do. The linemen get the least amount of attention and they appreciate that you know that about them. I liked it that they saw me as being like one of them. Those guys are just who I found myself ending up with all the time. It wasn't a conscious choice. It's just the way it was.

Chapter 9

The Freshman Starts

We traveled to Birmingham for our 1987 season-opening game against Alabama. As the team dressed in the locker room, Brett walked up to me with his uniform on and said, "Coach, I'm ready." I got a funny feeling when he said that. It was the same feeling I had when I first met Brett outside the field house at Hancock North Central High School. There is just no way to describe it. It's so intangible, just a feeling you get about a person who demonstrates complete confidence in his abilities. I quickly got over the feeling and came back to the reality that Brett never would see the field.

"All right, Brett," I told him. "All right."

Ailrick and Simmie split time at quarterback and we got handled pretty good, losing 38-6. As time in the game dwindled, I was hoping Jack would put Brett in. The game was out of hand, so what would it hurt? Brett never got in. I understood why. Jack hadn't given Brett any reps in practice to prepare for Alabama. Jack didn't want to embarrass Brett or our team. Things were embarrassing enough the way it was.

We had our usual staff meeting the next day to grade players and break down film on our next opponent, Tulane. We talked about the previous game and then discussed Tulane. As we finished the discussions, Coach Carmody mentioned again that he would like to see Brett get some game action. Jack reluctantly agreed.

Jack was in kind of a bind because he had spent so much time coaching Ailrick and Simmie in the spring and in two-a-days getting them ready to run the new offense. He didn't know what Brett was capable of doing. It was difficult to fathom that a true freshman would be able to execute the offense, in particular the quarterback position. Jack wasn't sure how serious Coach Carmody was about playing

> **Fact 4 Favre**
>
> Southern Mississippi retired Brett Favre's No. 4 in 1993.

69

(University of Southern Mississippi photo)

Brett Favre had his Southern Mississippi jersey No. 4 retired in 1993. The quarterback was inducted into the Southern Mississippi Hall of Fame in 1997 and named to the school's Football Team of the Century in 2001.

Brett and neither was I. As such, Jack didn't give Brett any reps as we prepared for Tulane.

The week flew by, as they tend to do during the season, and our home opener was upon us. We had a good week of preparation and we needed it. Tulane had an excellent, very athletic quarterback with the speed to run their option offense. He also threw very well and had outstanding receivers as targets. Tulane's head coach was Mack Brown, whom I had worked for at Appalachian State. Mack went on to be head coach at North Carolina and the University of Texas where he won the Bowl Championship Series National Championship in 2005.

On game day, we had position meetings, then the entire offense met as a group, as did the entire defense. We then had our pregame meal before heading to the locker room to dress for the game. Coaches made routine walks around the locker room, checking on their players. I made my walk, then headed for the coaches room to get dressed. Brett stepped right in front of me and it was a repeat of the Alabama pre-game.

"Coach McHale, I'm ready," Brett said. "I'm ready."

I have a little bit of a jokester side to my personality, so I said to Brett, "you'd better be ready. You'd better be ready because you're going to play today."

I have no idea why I responded that way. I didn't think Brett would get in the game, but it got Brett going pretty good.

"Oh shoot," Brett mumbled to himself. "Oh shoot."

Brett was all stirred up. I didn't let him know I was kidding him. It was just too much fun to see his reaction.

It was a terrific Saturday for football. The weather was beautiful and the setting was everything you'd want it to be. At halftime, we were tied, 14-14. Anyone with any football knowledge, though, could tell it merely was a matter of time before Tulane took over the contest. Their quarterback and receivers just had too much talent.

Our offensive staff met to make halftime adjustments. Ailrick and Simmie were having a very difficult time completing passes. Jack asked if I had any recommendations on changing blocking schemes or altering the game plan. All I could think of was how much trouble our quarterbacks were having and that Tulane wasn't having the same problem. I blurted that I didn't think any adjustments would make a difference and that we needed to put Brett in the game. I said it kind of harshly and I meant it.

 **Fact 4 Favre**

Brett Favre was named the Most Valuable Player in the All-American Bowl and the East-West Shrine game as a senior.

Just then, I saw a shadow on the wall. It was Coach Carmody's. I thought I was in deep trouble and that I would hear about it after the game. Just then, the officials came in to give us the five-minute warning to return to the field.

Tulane had the ball to open the third quarter and I was proven right. The Green Wave took the ball down the field and scored to take a 21-14 lead. We did nothing with the ball, throwing an incompletion that wasn't even close on third down before punting. Tulane again drove deep into our territory but this time we held them out of the end zone and regained possession. Again, we went three and out before punting. Our defense had been on the field a long time and was starting to wear down. The pendulum was swinging Tulane's way.

(Favre family photo)

It didn't take long for the media to put the spotlight on Brett Favre at Southern Mississippi.

Coach Carmody hollered for Brett.

"Take some snaps from center and warm up, you're going in," Coach Carmody told Brett.

Brett almost was in shock. I could tell he was really nervous.

"Oh shoot," Brett kept saying. "Oh shoot."

Tulane backed us up pretty good with a punt and Coach Carmody told Brett, "you're in."

I thought about how just two hours earlier I was kidding Brett about playing, never believing it for a minute. Now, here he was in the game. It was all so strange.

Brett got in the huddle and called a running play that gained a couple of yards. Jack called a pass on the next play. Brett dropped back, drifted a little to his right and was out of the pocket. I could tell he wasn't making a progression read with his receivers. He danced around a little and fired a rocket to an open receiver, drilling him right in the chest. There were only about 16,000 people in our 34,000-seat stadium, but each of them could hear the ball crack the receiver's pads.

Across the way, a small group of fans were making a lot of noise after that completion. It was the same group that heckled Irvin the first time I visited North Hancock. Except this time, Irvin was in the group, too, along with Bonita, Brett's grandmother, aunts and uncles. It was something to witness.

Brett drove the team down the field, completing all of his passes. He had no idea what the plays were, he just looked for open receivers, scrambled and completed passes. The drive ended with Brett throwing a touchdown pass, then throwing his arms into the air and jumping around. He was incredibly excited and his passion for the game was evident. More importantly, Brett was having great fun.

Coach Carmody was right, "Elway" got our defense excited. They played great when they saw how Brett was playing. We ended up beating Tulane by two touchdowns. I remember reading Mack Brown's comments in the newspaper the next day. He was asked if he had a game plan to stop Brett Favre's passing attack. Mack told the reporter he never had heard of Brett Favre and had no idea where he was from.

I've never seen, nor probably ever will see, anything like that again. Brett, a seventh-string 17-year-old, had earned the job as our No. 1 quarterback and started one week later against Texas A&M.

> **"Man does not see what the Lord sees, for man sees what is visible, but the Lord sees the heart." – I Samuel 16:7.**

BRETT'S VIEW

I probably was serious when I told Coach McHale I was ready to play against Alabama. I probably was, but realistically I didn't know I was. I didn't know what I'd be getting into. As the game was just about over, I was thankful I didn't get in. That would have been a bad one to start off in.

I remember, though, in pre-game warmups we were throwing fade routes and there were 85,000 people there. I knew that was where I wanted to be. I never thought twice about playing in the game. I didn't think I was going to play. I was just happy to be there.

In the locker room before the Tulane game, Coach McHale told me I'd better be ready because I was going to play. I thought he was just telling me what I wanted to hear. But up to that point, everything he'd ever told me pretty much had come true. He always shot straight with me. In the back of my mind I thought there was a chance and I thought I was ready, but what did that really mean?

When Coach told me to get ready because I was going in, I thought, "Oh boy, I'm getting what I asked for and I ain't ready for it." At first I thought I was going in to punt. I thought, "ain't no way," then I thought at least I was getting on the field. Then he told me to get loose because I was going in at quarterback. I knew that ready or not it might be the only chance I ever got. I knew I could go out, screw it up and be done forever or I might make a name for myself. I was scared to death. I had all these thoughts running through my mind. "What if I call the wrong play? What if I go the wrong way? What if the fans start booing me? What will the veterans say about me coming in?"

I remember being in the huddle and all five linemen were like 22 and I was 17. I don't remember the play I called, but I remember telling the guys we were going to go score. I thought I was going to lead us from behind, but I didn't know how. The rest was history, but it wasn't because I was the one who drew it up.

It was kind of like my first game in Green Bay. Some guys just wanted me to call the play and they were kind of content with losing. I think they thought, "what's this young kid going to do?"

I remember that game against Tulane. I didn't always know what the plays were. Numerous times there were seven-step drops and I took nine. One in particular we scored a touchdown. When we watched the film the next day, Coach White told me it was a good play but we didn't have any nine-step drops in the playbook. I was sitting there thinking, "Who cares? It was a touchdown."

It was to Chris Magee down in the broad corner of the end zone. I never thought about what to do if the defensive ends were in my face, what happened if the receivers were covered. I just thought it was my cup of tea. I was going to fake to the left, roll to the right and make something happen. I remember thinking this was going to be a touchdown. That, I was confident in.

If I'd had to draw back and make three reads, I wasn't ready for that but I knew I could make it work. My problem was when I saw he was pretty wide open I had to compose myself enough to get the ball to him. I was ready to celebrate even before the ball was snapped.

After that game I found out that Scott got thrown out because when I went in there was a big argument up in the stands. We talked about that. We talked about how this whole thing was too good to be true. It was way more than I was hoping for. I was hoping to make the traveling squad and if I got in, mop-up duty or whatever, that would be great. Never did I think I'd get in and lead our team from behind to win. Here I almost didn't get a scholarship and just hoped to make the traveling squad and the next thing I'm leading the team from behind as a 17-year-old in our first home game. Where did we go from there?

Chapter **10**

Favre 4 Heisman

Brett quickly continued his path toward success. He was developing into a quarterback who would get notice from the NFL and enhanced his reputation by playing well in big games. His most eye-catching performance came during his junior season when Southern Miss played Florida State in Jacksonville, Fla.

Southern Miss and Florida State had played one another for 20 years, alternating games at each school's home stadium. Southern Miss didn't draw well, even when Florida State came to town, so our Athletic Director, Bill McClellan, who had a great business mind, approached FSU about playing at a neutral site in Florida. Bill offered that Southern Miss would be willing to do it for $500,000. Bill had been athletic director at Clemson before coming to Southern Miss and knew a lot about striking deals on scheduling. He figured since Jacksonville was a short drive from Tallahassee, where Florida State is located, the potential deal would be attractive to the Seminoles. He was right. FSU agreed and we played our 1988 opener in Jacksonville.

A year earlier in Tallahassee, Florida State had beaten Southern Miss 49-13. That score suggests we took a beating, but our coaching staff saw it differently. We took a different approach to the loss and decided we could turn a negative into a positive. That's what coaches do in our psychological approach to athletes in trying to get any edge we can.

Our entire off-season effort was dedicated to beating Florida State. To convince our players that our plan wasn't just fantasy, our staff put together a project. We took game tape from the loss to FSU and cut out five key plays that contributed to the loss. One of those plays was of Brett throwing a pass that Deion Sanders intercepted in the end zone and returned for a touchdown. Another play cut out was a FSU pass on third-and-19. That pass just missed being deflected by Simmie Carter, who with Brett's success was moved to cornerback, and went for a touchdown.

We made two tapes for our players to study all summer. One was the game with the five plays cut out and the other was with the five plays left in. We noticed that we were getting the psychological results we were seeking. The players were beginning to believe the previous year's game with Florida State was a lot closer than the score indicated. Our guys were starting to exude confidence. We continually told them that if we played an error-free game, eliminating turnovers and big plays, we could at least make the game close. We never said we would win, just that the goal was to keep the game close into the fourth quarter. We figured if we could do that, Florida State might panic and give us a great chance to win.

Most national publications ranked Florida State No. 1 in the nation during the preseason. It seemed like every college football magazine featured a Florida State player on the cover with the words "National Champions" emblazoned everywhere. Several reporters wrote how FSU's easy opener with Southern Miss would help get the Seminoles started on their way to the national title. Based on the score of the previous year's game, that might have seemed like a natural assumption. The psychology we were using, however, set up a great opportunity to upset a powerhouse football program.

Fact 4 Favre

Brett Favre's 2.9 interception ratio (34 in 1,169 regular-season pass attempts) ranks among the best in NCAA history.

The summer went by quickly and our staff truly believed our team was capable of keeping the game close. Our game-week practices indicated that our players believed it, too. The contest was the only game televised that day and it was on national TV. Tom Curtis drove our bus, the "Eagle Express," the more than seven-hour haul to Jacksonville on Friday morning. Our budget didn't allow us to fly, but with the payout from this game we might be able to in the future. Many mid-major programs schedule games such as this, take a loss and collect a paycheck to boost the budget.

We settled in at the hotel, then headed for the Gator Bowl stadium so our players could get familiar with the field and locker room. The heat was stifling, even in shorts and T-shirts. We went through a mild workout and reviewed special teams substitutions, offensive and defensive personnel and bench control. The players' clothes were still sopping wet. I wondered how the heat would affect our team during the game. I hoped the weather would change.

We returned to the hotel for dinner and meetings to review the game plan. The game would kick off at 1 p.m. the next day, leaving us little time for details on game day morning. I noticed our players weren't showing the kind of nerves most teams do when taking on a top-ranked team. They were very businesslike. Brett, naturally, was as confident as anyone in his comments and actions.

The next morning, I stepped out of the hotel lobby to board the bus and sweat beads immediately popped out on my forehead. It wasn't just hot, it was torture. I sat next to a window on the bus and Tom had the air conditioning cranked as high as it would go. It didn't matter. We could see the moisture seeping through the thighs of our pants. By kickoff, this had to be one of the hottest days in history.

A sea of FSU garnet and gold greeted us at the stadium. They were doing the famous Seminole chop with their hands as we slowly approached our locker room. We were in a far-from-friendly environment that had to be intimidating for our players, the heat was unbearable and we were taking on the No. 1 team in the country.

I waited to let the players pass before I got off the bus. When Brett walked by he looked me square in the eye and said, "I'm ready, coach. I'm ready." He always said it and he always believed it. Brett was something else. They broke the mold after he was created. You had to love him. What a competitor! It transmitted to everyone around him.

> ### 🏈 Fact 4 Favre
>
> Brett Favre's 7,695 regular-season career passing yards ranks him among the top 30 in NCAA history.

About 90 minutes before kickoff our team walked onto the field and already there were people in the stands. I had observed our team in the locker room. The guys were unusually quiet. Was it nerves or was it a take-care-of-business attitude? Players were sweating as they put on their shoulder pads. One of our managers asked a trainer to find out the temperature. He came back and told us it was 110 degrees. I'd never coached in a game where it was that hot. This was going to be one for the books.

The locker room was getting stuffy. There was no air flow. We heard the crowd noise muffled through the walls and the national anthem began to play. The officials poked their heads in and asked for the captains to come out for the coin toss. That was my signal to head to the press box.

It was time. All the preparation had come to a close. Our team had its pre-game prayer and headed onto the field. The stadium was packed and the Florida State band was playing its famous war chant over and over. I took my place in the press box and looked to my left. Burt Reynolds, who had played at FSU in the mid 1950s, was sitting two boxes down. It was unbelievable. We were about to kick off to the No. 1 team in the nation and a former Seminoles' running back-turned-actor was in the press box to watch it. I placed my game plan sheets on the counter in front of me and thanked God they were laminated, as the sweat was dripping everywhere. How could those players in all that equipment handle this heat?

We kicked off and our defense played super, stopping Florida State on three downs and forcing a punt. Our offense marched the ball down the field, taking advantage of FSU's speed by running the inside zone play and cutting back against the pursuit. We drove to the 12-yard line but fumbled the ball away. I knew we wouldn't have many opportunities to score on those guys and turnovers would kill any chance we had of keeping the game close. Our players, though, were confident we could run the ball on such an outstanding defense and that confidence led to us taking a halftime lead.

On my way to the locker room at half, I noticed paramedics helping a woman onto a stretcher. She had passed out from the intense heat. Later, I learned that 10 people had been taken to the hospital to be treated for heat-related illnesses. In our locker room, several players were lying down and being given IVs to combat dehydration. Our team was in tremendous shape thanks to our conditioning program, but this was an unusually hot day for everyone. The room was quiet. We made our adjustments and emphasized our summer theme — keep the game close. We felt if it was close in the fourth quarter, we would win.

As I returned to the press box, all I could think about was whether our players could last four quarters in this heat. I knew Florida State had better depth and would continue to substitute players to keep them fresh.

In the second half, we were in control of the game until Florida State drove deep into our territory and attempted a field goal. One of our players broke through and blocked the kick. Another one of our players, Bryan McCloud, scrambled on all fours to scoop up the ball but unintentionally kicked it, advancing it 10 yards before we fell on it. Penalty flags rained down all over the field. I wasn't sure what the call could be, but at least we had possession of the football.

After a lengthy period, the officials decided that we had illegally advanced the ball after the block and recovery, so Florida State would retain possession with a 5-yard penalty added. I couldn't believe it!

Brett Favre holds five Southern Mississippi career offensive records and shares a sixth.

We blocked the kick, recovered the ball and the result is Florida State got the ball back five yards closer for another chance at the field goal. Unbelievable! FSU lined up again and kicked the ball, but it sailed wide right! What a break for us.

After the season, the NCAA changed the rule because of that play, altering it so that the defensive team would retain possession. That's the way the rule should be and it's how we thought it was originally. The officials made the correct call on a bad rule.

Eventually, Florida State took the lead with a few short minutes left. A field goal wouldn't do it for us. We had to drive the length of the field and score a touchdown to win. Our players, though, had done exactly what we'd asked them all summer to do — keep the game close into the fourth quarter.

We worked the ball down the field to the Florida State 30-yard line and faced fourth down. Brett threw an out cut and FSU's cornerback made an aggressive play, narrowly missing an interception. Had the corner simply knocked the ball down the Seminoles would have had the victory. Instead, the pass was completed and we had a first down inside the 20. The play was reminiscent of last year's game, except it was Florida State's corner rather than ours who barely missed a game-changing play.

We drove to the FSU 3, facing fourth-and-goal with seconds remaining. We had one shot to win this game. We called a play-action pass where Brett faked a run to his right and rolled to his left. Our tight end, Anthony Harris, ran a drag route across the middle from the right. Brett hit him right on target, a pass with perfect touch for a touchdown. We made the extra point and had the lead with 8 seconds left! If we could cover the kickoff and keep Florida State from scoring, we would have an improbable upset over the top-ranked team in the country.

Florida State wasn't about to give up. Rather than line up with the usual two kick returners, they lined up with four, two of whom were quarterbacks. Something was up. Trickery was in the air. We instructed our kicker to kick the ball high, so as to eat up time, and told our coverage team to break down in their lanes and let the returner come to them. We kicked the ball high and FSU fielded it at the 29. The returner ran to his right, then turned and threw the ball back across the field to his left. Our players had sprinted 30 yards and stopped, trying to keep Florida State in front of them. The Seminoles were throwing the ball all over the field, their receivers trying to get open. As I watched all this unfolding, I thought about how we hadn't prepared our team for this type of play. Obviously, Florida State had practiced for just this situation.

The play was continuing as the clock clicked to 0:00. The game, though, wasn't over until that play ended. All I could do was hold my breath. I could hear our coaches in my headset screaming to our players to stay right where they were. The crowd noise was deafening. All of a sudden, one of our players approached one of FSU's players who had just caught the ball. I was worried that that's exactly what the Seminoles wanted. We had worked so hard for this victory and now we were going to lose it on a trick play with no time on the clock. All the hard work, preparation and outstanding play in this tremendous game was about to slip away.

The FSU returner cocked his arm and threw the ball. My Adam's apple jumped up in my throat. The ball hung in the air in what seemed to be slow motion. The ball was coming down around our 10 and two of our players battled an FSU player for the ball. The ball bounced around a bit then hit the ground.

Game over!

We had just beaten the No. 1 football team in the country on national television. It didn't get any better than that. What a great game!

I hurried to the locker room to congratulate our players. I was anticipating the noise of celebration that accompanies a big victory, but when I got into the room it was dead quiet. Our players were so exhausted they didn't have the energy to celebrate. My eyes then caught the most precious picture I ever have witnessed in the game of football. Right in front of me was Chris Ryals, our big right tackle, sitting in an old, metal folding chair. His face was as red as if it had been sunburned. He was drenched with sweat and steam rose from the top of his head. Standing next to him was Brett, drained and rubbing the top of Chris' head. Their eyes met and in a moment that seemed to last forever, they mustered up their last bit of energy and said to each other, "we did it. We did it." The moment was priceless.

Two players who were roommates, from the same signing class, one who represented the team in the trenches, the other the leader of all, shared what this game was all about. They had nothing left to give and were victorious. Coach Vince Lombardi's famous quote ran through my mind:

"Any man's finest hour is the time he lays on the field of battle, completely exhausted, but victorious."

Not only were we victorious, David had just beaten Goliath. They will never forget, nor will I, that very moment in our lives.

Brett had a good game against a great defense. That game was the spark of a great junior season for Brett and he caught the eyes of NFL scouts. That the game was on national TV didn't hurt, as it boosted Brett's visibility.

The following spring, numerous scouts came to work him out. The unusual part was that several pro quarterback coaches came by for the workouts. Rumors persisted that he would be a first-round draft choice. We asked several of those coaches to come in and give our staff a mini-clinic while they were on campus. I remember June Jones from the Atlanta Falcons and Mike Holmgren of the San Francisco 49ers coming to talk with us after they worked out Brett.

Our sports information office was busy promoting Brett as a Heisman Trophy candidate. They made up a poster that featured the phrase, "Favre 4 Heisman." Brett was thinking of an NFL career and of how he needed to train himself for his senior season. Brett was in the best shape of his life and by the end of the summer he weighed 230 pounds. He was ready to enter his senior season looking like an NFL quarterback. He realized that a strong performance his senior year could be the difference in being a first-round pick or a second-rounder. That difference could be millions of dollars.

Brett returned home one weekend in July and went to a beach on the Gulf Coast to relax with some friends and family. "We were down there knocking around, enjoying ourselves, doing a little fishing," Brett's brother, Scott said.

Scott was driving behind Brett on their way home when a horrific site unfolded in front of him. Just a couple of hundred yards from Irvin Favre Road, Brett's car went onto the shoulder. Brett had overcompensated trying to get the car back on the road after taking a corner too fast and the vehicle flipped several times before slamming into a tree.

"That tree might have saved Brett's life," Scott said. "If he hadn't hit that, he probably would have rolled down into a ravine and into the water."

Scott raced to Brett's mangled car and saw that Brett couldn't get out on his own. Scott ran back to to his own car and got a golf club that he used to break a window and pull Brett out of the car.

"It's the best use I ever got out of a 9-iron," Scott said.

An ambulance took Brett to a hospital in Gulfport, Miss., before he was transferred to one in Hattiesburg. His thoughts were that his football career might well be over. His injuries were serious, but the doctors said he would recover. Whether he would play again, no one knew for certain.

While Brett was in the hospital, our team began two-a-day practices. I went to see him. He was lying on his back with all kinds of tubes protruding from his body.

"Oh, Coach McHale," Bonita said, as I entered the room. "This doesn't look good. All we ever worked for is over."

I'm not sure why, but my response wasn't the most consoling. I told Bonita I was ashamed of her for having such an attitude and that Brett would pull through, get back on the field eventually and get drafted. I didn't know any of that. I didn't even know what the doctors had said. I wanted to keep Brett's spirits up, though. I seized the opportunity to do just that when I noticed a small grease board on the wall of the hospital room. The staff used it for menus and such. I erased the menu and told Brett to push the button that allowed him to sit up in bed so he could read the board.

I told Brett what we had worked on that day in practice and I began drawing plays on the board. I turned to look at Brett and his eyes were wide open and getting bigger. He loves football and I was simply trying to give Brett and his family hope. I had no basis whatsoever to establish that he would ever run a play again. I was being selfish because I wanted it to be all right for the Favre family.

Brett got out of the hospital in time to attend the tail end of our summer practices. He didn't look good. His weight had dropped to 190 pounds and his uniform didn't fit properly. He didn't participate in any drills. All he could do was throw the ball around a little and jog when the other players did sprints. He had a long way to go.

Brett tried to eat at the training table in the dorm, but his food wouldn't digest properly and he couldn't keep it down. Brett went to our head trainer, Doc Herrington, and explained the problem. Doc immediately took Brett to a doctor who took X-rays. The pictures showed Brett had damaged his intestines. Apparently, the seat belt that saved Brett's life also had pinched his intestines shut. The doctor quickly scheduled Brett for surgery to remove a portion of the intestine then reattach it. While the procedure saved Brett's life, it made the outlook for his senior season appear extremely dismal.

After the surgery, Brett returned to practice about two weeks before our opener with Delta State. He was able to do very little and was on a slow pace. Because Brett was so good during his previous three years at Southern Miss, it was difficult for us to sign quarterbacks. They knew they wouldn't play much behind such a prolific player. Because of that, against Delta State we were going to start a walk-on named John Whitcomb.

It was a tough situation to put John in and our offense really struggled. Despite being a heavy favorite over Delta State, we won the game just 12-0. That didn't bode well for our second game. This was no Delta State. We were playing Alabama in Birmingham. It was Alabama's opener, so while we had one game under our belt, they had the advantage of having been able to scout us. Their coaches stayed around to see only the first half of our struggle against Delta State. They left at halftime, undoubtedly sure that we would pose no problem for them. I couldn't blame them. We knew upsetting the Crimson Tide would be nearly impossible.

Brett continued to practice that week and showed considerable progress. Still, he was a long way from being the Brett Favre of the previous season. We had a coaching change in the offseason that brought Curly Hallman to Hattiesburg. Curly kept our practices closed to the public that week to keep Alabama guessing who would play

(Favre family photo)

The Favre family made itself known throughout college football as it followed favorite son Brett during his career at Southern Mississippi.

quarterback. At our final practice that week, Curly surprised all of us by saying Brett would be the starting quarterback against Alabama. He didn't announce it to the press until we arrived in Birmingham. Even Irvin and Bonita didn't know. Our team had tremendous respect for Brett and Curly knew it. Starting Brett was a motivational tool.

We loaded up the bus and old Tom Curtis drove us to Birmingham. Our staff talked about a plan to rotate Brett in and out of the game, as he wasn't in condition to play the entire contest. He hadn't been exposed much to the heat and he hadn't practiced enough to be in football shape. Most of his training camp time was spent in bed in an air-conditioned hospital room. That he was on the field at all was amazing.

One of the Alabama coaches who had scouted us against Delta State was Ellis Johnson, who had been our defensive coordinator for a couple of years. He and I were close, so he stayed with me when he was in town. He had an offer to coach defensive ends at Alabama and this was going to be his first game with the Crimson Tide. Seeing him on my way up to the press box made for an odd feeling knowing I'd be coaching against an old buddy.

We played very conservatively, running the ball and playing for field position. We didn't ask Brett to throw much. The game was close in the second quarter and John Whitcomb was in the game. John took a snap and the ball flew through his hands and landed on top of his helmet. John was turning around looking for the ball. It wasn't funny to our coaches, but it had to be hilarious for every spectator in the stadium. John finally located the ball and fell on it. Since I was now the offensive coordinator, seeing such a fiasco made me very nervous, to say the least. John was under a lot of pressure, being a walk-on quarterback playing in front of 70,000 people at Legion Field. I just hoped he could hand off the ball so we could kill the clock. My instinct told me to put Brett in the game, but we had to stick with the game plan and save Brett for the fourth quarter if we could keep the game close.

Eventually, we got the break we needed. We punted deep into Alabama territory and the return man fumbled and we recovered. We ran the ball three straight plays, with Tony Smith finishing the short drive with a touchdown run off a toss sweep to give us a lead.

Legion Field's artificial surface was blazing hot, around 110 degrees just like Jacksonville's grass a year earlier. Because of the heat, we substituted our offensive line every third series. This tactic appeared to pay off, as Alabama's defense was tiring. That allowed us to run the ball and take time off the clock, a strategy that resulted in 27-24 victory. We had just beaten a program that would win the national championship one year later under Gene Stallings, a great coach.

It was a tremendous win and it didn't come because of the heroics of Brett Favre. The miracle win, though, was in great part because of the faith our players had in Brett. Our players truly believed that if Brett was playing we had a chance to beat any of the big guys. That certainly was true that day in Birmingham.

Our quarterback coach was sitting next to me in the press box that day in Alabama and as the final seconds ticked away, he looked at me and said, "this isn't supposed to be happening. This is Alabama, Hoss. Alabama." I told him you've just got to believe.

I don't know why, but the very first day I set my eyes on Brett and met him beside that little concession stand at HNC High School something in my spirit told me he was a guy who could lead Southern Miss over the big guys on our schedule. I was the proudest person in the profession and overly proud of the courage that Brett showed that day to his teammates. What a competitor!

Stallings summed up the effort in a comment during an interview looking back on that season: "You can call it a miracle or a legend or whatever you want to. I just know that on that day, Brett Favre was larger than life."

I hurried down to the elevator to get to the locker room to celebrate the huge win with our football team and to hug Brett. When the elevator door opened, there was Ellis.

"Great game, coach," Ellis said, lowering his head to stare at the floor.

I felt bad for Ellis. He had just left our program to go to a traditional power, then they lose their first game and he runs into me afterward. I know Ellis bounced back from it in a big way. He went on to become Alabama's defensive coordinator and helped them win that national championship.

We went on to have a good season. Our final game was at Auburn. It was another barnburner that went down to the last play. The 86,000 fans made it so loud that the press box vibrated. Our players couldn't hear Brett as he called the signals. I asked the coaches to call a timeout and to get Brett on the headsets. Even on the headsets we could hardly hear one another.

I asked Brett what play he liked and he said, "coach I want to run the naked play fake to the right and hit the tight end dragging to the left." I yelled into the headset that I had one better. We would run the same play, except call it with bootleg protection. Right guard Chafin Marsh was to pull in front of Brett for protection from the pass rush. I anticipated Auburn blitzing both outside linebackers to force Brett to throw before he wanted.

Brett agreed with me. He didn't care as long as he had this pass play. Brett called the play in the huddle and the offense went to the line of scrimmage. Brett moved up and down the line calling out the cadence. The ball was snapped and Brett faked a handoff to the running back on the right side before rolling to his left. Sure enough, the linebacker was blitzing and Chafin cut him down. Brett was on the move when he hit the tight end with a perfect pass for a touchdown.

The clock showed 0:00 and the scoreboard flashed Southern Miss 13, Auburn 12. It was another great win with the quarterback from Kiln, Miss. That victory helped us receive a berth to the All-American Bowl where we played North Carolina State. The announcement was made in the locker room right after the Auburn win. The All-American Bowl was to be played at a site all too familiar to us — Legion Field in Birmingham, Ala.

When the season ended, there was a lot of speculation that Brett's car accident might impact his draft status. He didn't have the stats he had earlier in his career because he missed one game and had started slowly while working himself back into shape. He was invited to the Senior Bowl and that would greatly increase his exposure for the draft.

Brett was leaving Southern Miss and leaving some great memories for our fans to cherish. He took Southern Miss to a higher level by leading them to great upset victories over some of the premier programs in the country. He was fun to watch because he had fun playing the game. Brett never was intimidated by anyone.

"I'm ready, coach. I'm ready," was his mantra. Brett always was ready. Everyone around him knew it. I was going to miss this guy tremendously.

> **"David defeated the Philistine with a sling and a stone..."**
> **– I Samuel 17:42.**

BRETT'S VIEW

I remember the wreck. Deanna and I were going to a movie that night and I was going home to take a shower. I was coming around a curve about a half-mile from the main road and Scott was behind me. I slid off the road and the next thing I knew when I came to was I thought I'd been in a plane crash. Scott busted the window with a golf club and crawled in the passenger side and dragged me out of the car. He didn't know if I was dead or alive. The car went off the right side of the road, went back across the left side over an embankment, flipped three times and hit a pine tree about 12 feet up before it slid down the tree and leaned against it.

I can remember the car flying and glass breaking and seeing trees and stuff. I remember Scott breaking the window but everything is kind of vague. I remember him screaming at me, "are you all right?" I told him I'd been in a plane crash because I'd remembered flying through the air and he told me I'd been in a car wreck. I had blood all up and down my left leg from where I hit my left knee. There's still a scar there. I had cuts all over me and my back was killing me. Both sides hurt, but my back really hurt.

I remember Mom was there and then the ambulance came. On the way to the hospital in Gulfport, 35 or 40 minutes away, I screamed with every bump we hit because it hurt so badly. I remember all the tests they did and I'd scream every time they moved me. I had fractured vertebrae, my arm was all purple and yellow from bruising. I had a concussion. My back still bothers me.

I'd lost 20 pounds from the wreck and then I couldn't eat, couldn't hold anything down. I looked terrible and felt like I was dying. When

I called our trainer to come get me and take me to the hospital, I was laid out on the floor in my underwear. I couldn't move. I was in really bad shape. I remember he put me in his van and I was hanging out the window throwing up blood the whole way.

The doctor who did surgery on me was George McGee. He told me he was going to cut me differently to do the least amount of damage then he told me I wouldn't be playing football this year. He told me how serious the surgery was, that he'd have to pull out my stomach and sit it on my chest to get to my intestines. It sounded awful. He was going over all of this stuff he was going to do and all I was thinking was, "I'm going to play this year." I didn't know how, but I was determined to play. I couldn't even straighten up my back, but if I could play after all this I could prove I could overcome anything. I had a redshirt year available to me, but I didn't want to take it. I don't know if there is a better way to show determination or stupidity.

By the time I came out of the hospital I'd lost 35 pounds and my back still hurt. They had to remove 20 inches of intestine. When I went back to practice, to say I was frail was an understatement. I was pale and my eyes were sunk back in my head. I just kind of half jogged on the sideline.

By the time we played Alabama, my uniform was falling off me. I think I had one touchdown pass, but it wasn't anything special. Just playing in that game gave me so much energy. Our guys were fired up about it and that meant more than any statistic. I didn't care if I threw four touchdown passes or one, as long as we beat them. That was big because they had been beating us pretty good in previous years.

It was like the Florida State game. I remember how hot it was, but I knew we were in good shape. We had run our butts off. What we lacked in depth we made up for in determination and hard work. I've had a chance to play with a lot of Florida State guys who were in that game and they said they figured it was a win for them. They said they figured they had so much more depth. I asked them if they ran after practice and they told me they never did because they had so much depth.

We were smaller and so much less talented than Florida State, but we were more determined. Every time they had a big play, we had one, too. We just kept returning the punches and kept hanging in there until some doubt crept into their minds and reassurance came to us.

After the game we were shocked. We just sent shock waves through the country. It will go down as one of the greatest wins I've ever been a part of.

Chapter 11

Once a mom, always a mom

Bonita Favre is a special woman. She had a lot to do with the way Brett turned out. I think she was kind of the disciplinarian in the home and she had a lot of influence on the kids. She's smart and feisty, and I think some of that rubbed off on Brett. I think she believes that Scott could have been just as successful athletically as Brett was had the circumstances been just right.

"I knew a little bit about recruiting because of Scott, but not much," Bonita said. "I remember the recruiter coming from Mississippi State to see Scott and I remember them taking us to dinner, but it was different than it was with Brett. I'm a firm believer that as successful as Brett's been, you still have to be in the right place at the right time and be prepared. There are a lot of athletes who never get a chance and they're good athletes."

> **Fact 4 Favre**
>
> Brett Favre threw 20 or more touchdown passes in 12 straight NFL seasons (1994-2005). His 19 games with four or more TD passes trails only Dan Marino's 21.

Bonita wanted Brett to go to Southern Miss. She knew it was a good fit from the outset.

"Let's say that Brett went to Florida State," Bonita said. "He might never have gotten off the bench. You know, the Lord has blessed him. Brett was where he needed to be every time and he was prepared."

Being a coach's wife is hard enough. If you don't believe me, just ask Beverly. She'll tell you. How she puts up with me, I don't know. Being a wife of a coach whose children play for him is doubly tough. Bonita knew that well. She knew people said things about Brett. She heard the whispers and the murmurs.

"People used to say my kids were quarterbacks and pitchers because their dad was the coach," Bonita said. "Well, that's true, but he worked them twice as hard, too. When the team left the football field, it was over for the other players. Not for our kids. He'd have them out in the

(Photo by Beverly McHale)

Bonita Favre believes fate smiled on son Brett, but the player's talent, hard work and persistence were the reason he made the most of the unlikely chance he received with his scholarship to Southern Mississippi.

yard. He'd have them running that road."

Bonita saw Brett develop as a person and as an athlete. She knew he had great ability, but she couldn't gauge exactly how much. Scott had been a terrific athlete, too. Brett had tremendous confidence in his own ability and had a way of making things happen. Whether he could make his dream of playing in the NFL take place, though, wasn't something Bonita had an early handle on.

Sure, Brett was a star, but he was a star of a small-school football team. Recruiters hadn't exactly flocked to him. If colleges weren't calling, pro football seemed like nothing more than a mere dream, a dream shared by thousands of high school boys throughout the country. Brett was a football standout, but he also was her little boy, no matter how big and tough he was.

"I get asked by people if I knew Brett was going to be a super hero," Bonita said. "Now, how could I know that as a mother? I knew he was talented, but all my boys were talented. I just went with the flow and never even thought about it."

Brett thought about it, but it wasn't the Green Bay Packers green and gold he envisioned himself wearing after college. He had his heart set on silver and blue.

"From fifth grade on, Brett said he was going to play for the Dallas Cowboys," Bonita said. "He's a hard-headed one, so when he said something you usually should believe it."

Bonita has fun watching Brett play in the NFL. She had just as good a time piling in the van with family members and trekking to high school fields across Mississippi to see him play.

"My mom went," Bonita said. "My brothers and sisters, aunts, uncles, cousins went. Aunt Lane and Uncle Tim, cousins Danielle and Chase went. David Peterson and his wife Kristy went, too. Janlynn, who is another cousin, went. My friend Pat from New Orleans and her kids used to come. It was nothing for us to have 30 people there."

All 30 thought they knew more than Irvin and they let him know it. Bonita knew the life of a coach. After all, she was one, having coached girls basketball at North Gulfport Middle School.

"You know, there's a fine line between being a coach's wife and varsity mother," Bonita said. "You have to look at both sides of the fence. I knew Brett could throw the ball, but he didn't get to."

Fact 4 Favre

Brett Favre started his first game at quarterback for the Green Bay Packers on Sept. 27, 1992.

There was tension between Irvin and Brett and Bonita knew it. The reason was play calling. Scott never would have questioned his dad. Brett wasn't one to keep his feeling in check quite so much.

"One time at Pass Christian, I'll never forget it," Bonita said. "Irvin called a play and Brett ran something else and scored a touchdown. Irvin and Brett got in each other's faces. Some of the assistants had to get between them. Brett had scored a touchdown and he was proud of that, but he had run the wrong play and Irvin didn't like it."

Bonita knew that Brett was capable of making big plays with his arm. She sometimes was frustrated that he didn't get to throw more.

"Brett had an eye for the field," Bonita said. "For some reason he can see all that field and he could in high school, too. He'd see the field and change a play on his own and his dad would get furious."

Brett's example rubbed off on the rest of the siblings. Jeff got even braver than Brett and then Brandi wanted to play quarterback, too. Of course, Irvin and the boys wouldn't let her.

"Brandi would tell her dad that she could beat any of those wussies he had out there playing for him," Bonita said. "Growing up with the boys, she probably could have. They played rough. There was never a dull moment."

There was never a dull moment for Bonita in Benny French's Tavern, either. The bar where Bonita and Irvin stayed in the mid-1970s was a playground of adventure for Scott and Brett.

"We had living quarters, but it was loud," Bonita said. "The boys had the run of the place. Brett doesn't even eat Reeses Peanut Butter Cups any more because he ate so many there. They'd get in the sandwiches and chips."

And an occasional sip of Dixie Beer?

"I wouldn't doubt that either," Bonita said. "When Scott was really little, Mom heard a noise and she found Scott sitting on the floor popping all the tops on the beer."

As a teacher, Bonita was the ultimate utility player. Not only did she coach, she taught a variety of subjects, including biology, drug education, physical education, English and special education. At various points she went back to college and earned a Masters degree.

The special education classes were challenging, as Bonita felt like she didn't

> **Fact 4 Favre**
>
> Brett Favre signed a "lifetime" contract with the Green Bay Packers on March 1, 2001.

know what she was doing. She had a heart for those kids, however, and so do her children.

"I firmly believe the Lord will put you where you need to be," Bonita said. "Brett majored in special ed. Scott's degree is in special ed. Brett's wife Deanna was my aide in special ed. It grows on you, but you either love it or you hate it."

Bonita loved it. She's about as proud of some of her students as she is of her own children, including Brett.

"I have kids I taught who are out there working now that you never would have thought could be," Bonita said. "No one would have given them a chance years ago. I'm very proud of them. It's very rewarding. My kids grew up going to Special Olympics and being around the special ed kids. It was the best thing I ever did in my teaching career. Some people told me not to do it, but I loved it."

Brett said academics weren't his strong point in college, but Bonita said he was being modest. Brett was a strong student in high school.

"Brett would never bring home a book and he'd still get all As and Bs," Bonita said. "I'd ask his teachers how he did it and they told me he would listen and retain. All of my kids were different in school and you can't compare them."

(Perry McIntyre/Getty Images)

The Atlanta Falcons and Head Coach Jerry Glanville selected Brett Favre in the second round of the NFL Draft in 1991.

Bonita doesn't compare them as adults, either. She said it's not fair to anyone.

"It was difficult with my kids with their brother being a star," Bonita said. "People think because Brett is a millionaire that all my kids are. Brett is very generous and very giving. He's helped out, but it's not his duty to take care of us. All of the kids have their own jobs and live within their means."

(Drew Hallowell/Getty Images)

Brett Favre quickly became known for his toughness under pressure. He always has seemed to find a way to make a play for his team. Favre became the NFL's career leader in touchdown passes in the fourth game of the 2007 season when he threw his 421st to move out of a tie with former Miami Dolphin's great and Hall of Famer Dan Marino.

Multitudes of players say the NFL isn't as fun as college or high school football because it's a job. With Brett, pro football doesn't seem like a job. He enjoys himself on the field, smiling and jumping around having fun. Brett always has been that way.

"Brett had that competitive side, but he had fun," Bonita said. "I remember in Little League kids wouldn't hit against him because he might strike them out or he might knock them out. Even now, when I watch him on the field, I see that little 10-year-old kid with the fire and the excitement. He's so unpredictable."

Unpredictable. That's a good word to describe Brett and his journey from Rotten Bayou to the NFL. No one knew how things were going to turn out. No one really even knew the next step in the process of recruiting him. For a while, after the car wreck, no one even knew if Brett would live.

"We were at a church function," Bonita said, remembering the accident. "We got the news and my nephew David drove me to the scene. We must've been going 100 miles per hour. At first, we went to the wrong place.

"When we finally got to the right place, I ran down there and Scott told me Brett was 'all right,' meaning he was alive. I rode with Brett in the ambulance and he asked me if I thought he'd ever get to play football again. Of course, I didn't want to tell him that I didn't know."

Of course Brett did play again and made it to the NFL with Atlanta before being traded to Green Bay.

"I remember coming home from school and puttering around in the kitchen and Brett and Jeff were sitting there eating crawfish," Bonita said. "They were talking about how cold it got in Green Bay and I asked them what they were talking about."

"I got traded to Green Bay today," Brett said.

Bonita's response was, "where's Green Bay."

Irvin and Bonita visited Green Bay with Brett's agent, Bus Cook. The trio were in a taxi and Bus decided to mess with the driver, asking him what he thought of the new kid the Falcons had just traded to the Packers.

Fact 4 Favre

Brett Favre entered the 2007 NFL season with the league record for career pass completions with 5,021.

"That cab driver said he thought the Packers had lost their minds," Bonita said. "He said he didn't know what they were thinking. A lot of people thought that way because Brett was an unknown."

Bonita said she is proud that Brett has remained humble. She said he often takes the blame for an incomplete pass or interception after a receiver has run the wrong route.

"That goes back to that teamwork that was instilled in him way back in Little League baseball," Bonita said. "Brett's never thought anything of going and throwing a block and things like that. He's going to do what he has to do for the team. His daddy taught him that. Brett respected him for that."

Bonita is all mom, right to the end. While fans might like to see Brett go out with a Super Bowl victory, Bonita hopes he makes it through what might be his final season without getting hurt.

"I know he'll be in the Hall of Fame and all that," she said. "I pray that everybody stays healthy and Brett has a good, injury-free end to his career."

Brett hopes so, too. Of course, he wants another Super Bowl ring to go with his first one.

"I've had a great career," Brett said. "It's been more than I ever imagined. I have so many people to thank for that. I've really been blessed and I know that. I'm ready for whatever happens next."

(Favre family photo)

Brett and wife Deanna with daughters Brittany, left, and Breleigh. Brett and Deanna were high school sweethearts.

"Do nothing out of selfish ambition or vain conceit, but in humility consider others better than yourself." — Philippians 2:3.

BRETT'S VIEW

Mom wanted what was best for me and for all of us kids. She used to get on Dad to let me throw the ball more, but it worked out pretty good for me.

She was always leading that group of family that came to all the games. Was I aware of them? Oh, gosh, yeah I was aware of them. I knew they were there and I'd hear them getting on Dad about the play calling and all that.

After games I'd ride home with Mom because Dad would still be at the field washing uniforms until 11 o'clock or so at night. There were always discussions during the ride home. We'd talk about the game and how I played or college and this and that.

Mom was always there, always involved. We got a lot of our personality from her. I think she was competitive, just like Dad was. She encouraged us and kept us in line and all of that kind of stuff. She was good with the kids. She kept us humble. People probably think

I'm something because of the Super Bowl MVP thing. The thing I'm probably the most proud of about my career and about where I am today is that none of that stuff has ever bothered me. I'm proud of it and all, but I don't go hob-knobbing around with people because of it.

People meet me and they tell me they thought I'd be different. I hear that from people. They say they thought I'd act like I'm some superstar. I don't want to act that way. I just want to blend in. When I go watch one of Brittany's basketball games, I'm not there for people to see me, I just want to blend in and be treated like everyone else. I wanted the people to say I was just like them.

It's like when I'd go up to Oak Grove High School to work out. I'd get there about 8 in the morning and maybe talk a little football with the coaches. I was impressed that at 8 in the morning there would be kids already there lifting weights and working out. I'd go in and work out with them. My lifting days are pretty much over, but I'd go throw and run with them. It was fun. They never came up and asked for autographs or anything. I don't know if someone told them not to or told them I wouldn't sign or something, but they were nice people.

Afterwards, we'd go in and talk shop a little bit. They'd ask what we planned at Green Bay against this defense or that defense. I had a blast talking to the coaches and all those guys.

People ask me if after I retire I might like to go in to coaching. There is no way I'd get into coaching in the college or in the pros. It's just too much time. You make decent money, but it's just your quality of life. It's always the next job and there's all that recruiting that you have to do. It's the same thing with these pro guys. You don't have to worry about the kids being in class and stuff like that, but you're constantly breaking down film, even in the offseason. Shoot, there's no way. I like my free time too much for all that.

I might not mind volunteering a little somewhere or something like that, but I don't want to be employed by a school because I don't want someone telling me I have to do this or that. Helping out with the developmental stage is all right. In college you can kind of develop players, the way he draws back his arm, the way he blocks, things like that. You can make players a little bit better. In ninth or 10th grade, though, you can develop a guy's arm strength in a different way or you can give him tips and stuff like that that will make a big difference. I enjoy that. I don't want something where I have to be there every day.

I want to spend time with my family and do some things I like to do. That's what I look forward to doing.

(James V. Biever/Getty Images)

Brett Favre said his father Irvin was there to coach him every day until his death in 2003.

Chapter 12

Brett Keeps No. 4

After the All-American Bowl, Brett was invited to the Senior Bowl in Mobile, Ala., and to the East-West Shrine Game in Palo Alto, Calif. Brett didn't play well in the Senior Bowl but in the East-West Shrine Game he was named the co-player of the game.

Brett continued to train and prepare for the NFL. The Favre family invited me to join them for a draft party at their home. I drove the familiar route from Hattiesburg to Kiln, reminiscing about the many recruiting trips made through that territory. I wondered what round Brett would be drafted in and which team would draft him. He'd had a unique senior season. His stats were down, thanks to the car accident. How would that affect an NFL team considering taking him and plugging him in to the most important position on the field?

I thought Brett was worthy of the first round, but I was prejudiced. He proved he could play and succeed against tough opponents. Balancing out his statistical drop was the incredible toughness he displayed after having a foot of his guts removed just before the season. Draft day was going to be interesting.

Fact 4 Favre

Brett Favre became the winningest quarterback in NFL history when Green Bay defeated the New York Giants 35-23 in the second game of the 2007 season. The victory was Favre's 149th in the league, moving him out of a tie with John Elway.

It was a beautiful April day as I turned down Irvin Favre Road toward the family's home. A large crowd of people gathered in the yard next to Rotten Bayou. I recognized most of them as "the clan" I had seen at that first high school game I saw Brett play. He had such great support from his family and friends. This was another big day, the latest in a long line of them. The scene reminded me of what the family must have looked like when he received the phone call that he had received a scholarship from Southern Miss.

(Photo by Beverly McHale)

Brett Favre is the only player in NFL history to win three straight Associated Press Most Valuable Player awards.

This time, the call would deliver not a scholarship but a large sum of money. The difference between the first round and the second round was considerable. We talked about that as I sat in a chair next to Irvin overlooking the bayou. We talked about the days when I recruited Brett and about the great victories he led at Southern Miss.

The first round came and went without Brett being selected. Every team had passed on him. I wonder if they think much about that now, about what might have been. Finally, the phone rang and it was a representative of the Atlanta Falcons, who had selected Brett in the second round with the 33rd pick overall. Ironically, Ron Wolf of the New York Jets was set to take Brett with the next pick. Ron went on to become the general manager of the Green Bay Packers in November of 1991.

When Brett came out of the house to tell us Atlanta had drafted him I was a bit concerned. I knew of their head coach, Jerry Glanville, and their offensive coordinator, June Jones. I spent time visiting with June in the old USFL and I knew what kind of offense he ran. It was known as the "run-and-shoot" and I didn't think Brett was a good fit for that style of offense. When I was at the Senior Bowl I talked with an assistant from the Denver Broncos concerning NFL quarterbacks. He told me it took quarterbacks about three years to learn the system at that level and that if they were asked to play much before that it could ruin them.

Fact 4 Favre

Brett Favre was named one of Sports 100 "Good Guys" by The Sporting News in July 2000 in recognition of his civic responsibility and character. Favre's "Brett Favre Fourward Foundation" was established in 1996 and through that and other efforts, the player has raised tens of millions of dollars for charity.

I waited for the opportune time to sit down and congratulate Brett and pass on the wisdom I had gleaned from the Broncos coach. I was well aware of the confidence Brett exuded and that he would be thinking he was ready to start for the Falcons. I could hear him now, "I'm ready, June. I'm ready." I told him he would need to be patient. That's the last piece of advice I gave Brett before he left for Atlanta.

Brett was able to keep his jersey No. 4 with the Falcons and he kept that number after he was traded to Green Bay. We separated paths for a while as I took various coaching jobs in the World Football League, the Canadian Football League and at the collegiate level. Because of my busy schedule, breaking down film on Sundays, I rarely got to see Brett play.

I got to see him live, though, when I was coaching in the WFL. Our season was in the spring and part of my job was evaluating NFL players in the fall for our draft. The league mailed me a beta projector with the tapes of all the NFL exhibition games. A certain number of players were allocated to our team and we drafted the rest. I was in hog heaven having all those NFL games in my living room to study not only the players, but the offensive schemes of each team. I was especially excited looking at Green Bay tapes. I got to watch Brett, who played the first half of most of those exhibitions.

That fall, Green Bay was playing the Saints in New Orleans. I called Chet Franklin, who was in player personnel for the Saints to get tickets for my wife, Beverly, and me. Chet was our general manager when I worked for the Montreal Machine in the WFL. Beverly and I were living in Hattiesburg, so it wasn't a long trip to New Orleans. We got there early to walk around the French Quarter, visit the antique shops and see Bourbon Street. Walking around, we saw numerous Packers fans. They were easy to spot because so many were wearing green and gold No. 4 jerseys. It was a funny feeling seeing all of those jerseys with Brett's number, knowing I had recruited and coached him. It made the trip very special for me. I was excited to get to the Superdome and see him in person.

Fact 4 Favre

Brett Favre broke a tie with George Blanda for most career interceptions thrown when he suffered his 279th in the sixth game of the 2007 season.

When we got in the dome, memories flooded back. I had coached several college games in the Superdome while at Southern Miss when we played Tulane. Brett had some good games against Tulane. Beverly and I made it to our seats and it felt odd to be a spectator watching Brett play rather than his coach.

I looked around the dome and noticed how high the scoreboard hung over the middle of the field. It dawned on me that Ray Guy, who was on our staff at Southern Miss while Brett was there, used to punt for the Oakland Raiders. Ray once had hit that scoreboard with a punt. I remember watching Ray punt when I was in high school. He was the best I'd ever seen, but to have hit the scoreboard in the Superdome was unfathomable.

The game got under way and I could hardly contain my excitement for seeing Brett play. I was eager to see Reggie White, the Packers great defensive end, play too. Being an offensive line coach, I paid special attention to Reggie working against the Saints' left tackle when Green Bay was on defense. I knew he was setting up that poor guy for the fourth quarter with his pass rushing technique. Reggie bull-rushed that guy all day until the Packers needed a big play and he used a spin move to make a critical sack and force the Saints to punt.

As I watched Brett, it was just like watching him when he was in college. He threw a touchdown pass very similar to the one he threw for us against Tulane. It was a deep corner route and was very hard to explain other than it was like deja vu for me.

Green Bay won the game and Brett was outstanding. I had to have been the proudest person in the Superdome. I told Beverly that we were going down to the Green Bay locker room and look up Brett. When we got there, the press was all over him. There were lights, cameras and microphones everywhere. As Brett was being interviewed, he spotted me out of the corner of his eye. He didn't know I was going to be there.

Brett excused himself from the press and came over to Beverly and me. He looked back to the press and told them, "this is the guy who recruited me in college." That was a special moment for me. That's the kind of person Brett is. It was important to him to recognize me that way and that's part of what makes Brett Brett.

 **Fact 4 Favre**

Brett Favre threw a touchdown pass in 16 straight postseason games (1994-2005). His 34 TD passes in postseason rank second to Joe Montana's 45.

As Beverly and I drove home, we discussed what a great day it had been. That was when she encouraged me to write a book about my experiences recruiting Brett. I'd never thought much about it before, but why not. It's a great story of how Brett went from right across Lake Ponchatrain to Southern Miss to the NFL and had developed into a superstar.

I moved on from the WFL and landed a job at Marshall University in Huntington, W.Va., where I had the opportunity to work for one of the winningest coaches in college football. Bob Pruett was the head coach at Marshall, and the Thundering Herd won more games in the 1990s than any other NCAA Division I program in the country.

While at Marshall, I was fortunate to work with another outstanding quarterback, Byron Leftwich, who went on to become a first-round draft pick and starter with the Jacksonville Jaguars. Byron had a lot of pressure on him at Marshall because he replaced Chad Pennington, a Heisman Trophy finalist, first-round draft pick and starter with the New

York Jets. Byron handled it well and became a star of his own.

My recruiting area at Marshall was Mississippi and Alabama. I was doing some recruiting along the Gulf Coast of Mississippi in 2003, right after our regular season had ended and just before our bowl game. I went by a couple of high schools and the coaches, kind of like they did when they asked me if I had seen Brett play, asked me if I had been to Favre's restaurant. I didn't even know Brett had a restaurant. I got directions and discovered it was along the highway to his home in Kiln.

I couldn't reach Irvin on the phone, so I just drove to the restaurant and hoped I would get to see Irvin and Bonita later. Brett, of course, was in Green Bay. I saw the sign — "Favre's on the Bayou" and pulled in the parking lot. I went inside and asked for Irvin. The manager, who I didn't know, told me Irvin wasn't there and he came around every once in a while. I asked the manager to call Irvin and tell him I was there. He did and Irvin came right over. It was good to see him again. We had dinner and talked about how far Brett had come since the days when he was being recruited.

Irvin and I talked for about two hours. He told me he had suffered several heart attacks but didn't tell his family about them. He told me he had been visiting the priest at his church for several weeks. I told Irvin he simply had to tell his family about his heart problems, that he had no choice.

"I know," Irvin said. "I just don't want them to worry about me with Brett playing up there in Green Bay. I don't want it to affect his playing."

About that time, Bonita, Scott, Brandi and Lane came in the door. We sat around and had a great time talking about the past. I wanted to stay there all night, but I had to be in northern Mississippi to recruit the next day. It was going to be a long trip as it was, so I said my farewells and headed north.

Irvin had given me a big scare and couldn't talk more about his heart problems because the family walked in. I said a prayer for Irvin as I was driving and hoped he was all right. Little did I know that visit would be my last with him. That December, Irvin died.

I had spent a great deal of time with Irvin while recruiting Brett and we'd gotten close. After I left Southern Miss to coach at the University of South Carolina, I got a call at home from Irvin. To his surprise, a female voice answered. Irvin asked if he could speak to me and was told I wasn't home, yet. Irvin asked if she was the housekeeper. Beverly shot back, "no, I'm his wife." What followed was classic Irvin.

"Hey Bonita," Irvin said. "McHale has a damn wife!"

Irvin didn't know I had gotten married that summer. He knew me when I was single at Southern Miss. Beverly never will forget that call. We all were going to miss Irvin.

Beverly and I made the trip to Pass Christian, Miss., for Irvin's funeral. So many people attended the service some of them had to stand outside the church. It was football season and Brett and his head coach Mike Sherman and many of the Packers showed up to support him.

Green Bay's next game was with Oakland. Brett was torn between staying home with his family and getting back to play that game. Brett decided to play the game because his dad would have had it no other way. I couldn't watch the game because I was on a recruiting trip, but I remember seeing the highlights. Brett had one of the best games of his career and the Packers beat the Raiders 41-7. I saw the emotion that filled Brett that night and know that he truly believed that Big Irv was watching his son play from above. I believe that, too.

Irvin was special, but so is Bonita. She quit coaching to stay home and raise children. She did a heck of a job with all of them. All turned out to be great athletes and I think her toughness at home with the kids had a lot to do with that.

> **"I have fought the good fight. I have finished the race. I have kept the faith." – II Timothy 4:7.**

BRETT'S VIEW

People talk about me winning three MVP awards, but someone will break that record. It's like any other record. It's just a matter of time. I never thought I'd get three, so it might take a while, but someone will get four.

Winning a Super Bowl, nine Pro Bowls, three MVPs, I tell people all the time this has been way more than I ever thought of. I'd always dreamed I'd play and always thought I would, but what guy doesn't? I never thought I'd be the MVP. I mean, that's the best player in the NFL.

It's been great. I'd like to go out with a Super Bowl win, but what the average fan doesn't understand is that to win the Super Bowl you have to have the right pieces to the puzzle — the right players, make the right trades, have some luck. A lot of luck. Maybe you get a field goal to win a road game you would have lost. There are a lot of plays you

(Photo by Beverly McHale)

The Green Bay Packers reserved a game ball for Irvin Favre from their 41-7 victory against the Oakland Raiders. Favre died of a heart attack the day before the game, but Brett went ahead and played in the game, passing for 399 yards and four touchdowns.

run and sometimes they work and sometimes the same play doesn't.

I've had a great career. I've done it all, which is more than I ever set out to do. I've achieved every team and individual honor there is to achieve, so from that standpoint, there's nothing left to prove. I've always wanted to give my team the best chance to win. I've never wanted to sit and watch.

Each year is a challenge. The challenge in the 2006 season was greater because we were so young. We had the youngest team in football and it didn't look like that would change for 2007. I'd like for those young guys to be able to say I taught them a lot, that I was a competitor and that I was fun to play with. That means something to me.

It's special to have spent so much time with Green Bay. I think what I've accomplished is rare. I think I'm as determined as any guy who has ever played, but I can't say there hasn't been someone who has been as determined, if not more. I can't say that sets me apart. Luck played a big part in it. I think my work ethic has been unmatched and the people of Green Bay appreciate that. I think NFL fans period appreciate the way I approach the game and the way I play. Whether they like me doesn't really matter.

There were a lot of good players who came before me and more will come after me in Green Bay. There's so much history and tradition there. I'm well aware of what tradition means. From the time I could pick up a football I watched games and read up on guys and knew statistics. I could tell you pretty much every player on every team. I couldn't tell you where Green Bay was, but I could tell you what type of football team they had and I could tell you about a lot of their players.

Playing in Green Bay never has gotten old. You go into that town and there are 100,000 people. Some stadiums hold that. The Packers have a 40-year waiting list for tickets and you never see an empty seat. That stadium has been there 50 years and there have been some renovations, but the places where those guys scored touchdowns, walked out of the tunnel, even parked their cars, has remained the same. As I get older and look back it will be even more special, but

 **Fact 4 Favre**

Brett Favre moved out of a second-place tie with Mick Tinglehoff for NFL consecutive games played in the fourth game of the 2007 season. Favre, the only non-lineman among the top five in the category, had 241 to trail leader Jim Marshall by 29 games. In 2004, USA TODAY named Favre "The Toughest Athlete in Sports."

not one day has gone by when I thought this wasn't as a big a deal as I thought it was going to be.

I've played 16 years. Most guys don't get to do that. Some of them throw away the opportunity. They don't appreciate the opportunity they have. I love football. You can't fake that and it shows. If you look at it as a job and a grind then it does become a long year and it does become tough. There are times in meetings or in practice maybe, but you know I have it pretty good when they pay me to do this. I like the fame and all that stuff, but I love throwing a touchdown pass. You can't put a price on that and I can't explain to someone what that feels like.

People probably assume that I don't get tired of throwing them and that every time I complete a pass I get excited. There will come a time when that's not the case and somebody else is going to be doing it, so I'm trying to enjoy it as much as I can.

It's no different than anyone else. You do something for a certain period of time and you get bored with it. Off the field, I like working on my property. A storm comes through and knocks down trees or something and it seems everything you've worked for is wiped away, but those are challenges you face all the time.

As for the Hall of Fame, this might sound crazy, but I'm aware of it and I jokingly tell Deanna all the time that I'm going to be the first guy to accept being inducted via satellite from my own property. I get uncomfortable going to do things like that. To me, the reward was playing. I don't need someone to make a statue of me or put me in the Hall of Fame to put the icing on the cake.

That's not being disrespectful or anything like that. I'm just content with my career and maybe it will all mean something more later on down the road. I think my career speaks for itself. The Hall of Fame is obviously special, but it reaffirms your career. I don't think I really need that. I'm not saying I wouldn't go, of course, but just playing the game was way more than enough.

I have to thank Dad. He'd come up to Green Bay for a game and throw his two cents worth in. I'd just listen. He didn't know anything about a passing game. He watched the games on TV and would call me and tell me what he thought. He coached me until the day he died.

Epilogue

Anyone who knows Brett Favre will tell you that nobody relishes a challenge more than this guy. The longer the odds or the darker the situation, the quicker his competitive juices start flowing. And they've been flowing since he was old enough to walk and hold some kind of ball. Having an older brother who wants to keep you in your place will do that.

As a youngster, Brett had to work hard to escape Scott's shadow. When he did that, he had to prove to his Hancock North Central High School teammates and their families that he wasn't the baseball team's starting pitcher or the football team's starting quarterback just because his dad was a coach at the school. He had to prove he truly was the best player at the position — and he did.

His goal of playing college football was toughened by the fact he was a quarterback in a running offense at a small school in an out-of-the-way location. No one can honestly say Brett would have had a chance to play college football had that rival coach not tipped me off about him. And even then, my first couple of visits were more courtesy than sincere scholarship recruiting interest.

Fact 4 Favre

Antonio Freeman has been Brett Favre's favorite receiver on touchdown passes. The two have connected 57 times.

Even when it became apparent to me that Brett could help Southern Mississippi, I still had to tell him and his family that despite my belief, the deck was stacked against him that a scholarship would be waiting on National Signing Day. A lot of things had to fall into place for Brett to have the opportunity to receive a grant from USM, but somehow they all did. Kids back out on commitments to schools at the 11th hour of Signing Day year in and year out, but the player who benefits from the reversal of field by another seldom possesses Brett's talent.

It was that talent that enabled him to again beat the odds and make the most of his unlikely opportunity with USM. The last of seven quarterbacks on the pre-season depth chart — and not our top fresh-man quarterback recruit at that — Brett wound up being the school's first four-year starter at the position, an All-American and a legend in Golden Eagles' lore.

To that point, Brett's physical skills had pretty much been the equal-izer for him to balance the playing field. But once in the NFL, it was his mental toughness that surfaced so many times to enable him to deal with adversity, particularly away from the field.

Consider in the span of 20 months from late December 2003 to late July 2005, Brett lost Big Irv to a heart attack, his brother-in-law Casey in an ATV accident on Brett's property in Mississippi, Deanna developed breast cancer and his childhood home was destroyed by Hurricane Katrina.

It takes someone with a men-tal focus bestowed on few to not only continue at the game's high-est level but thrive. In the 2004 season, which was punctuated by Casey's death and Deanna's diag-nosis in a week's time in October, Brett compiled some of the best statistics of his life. He completed 346 of 540 passes for 4,088 yards with 30 touchdowns and only 17 interceptions. His 64.1 completion percentage was the second-best of his career and his 92.4 rating was

 **Fact 4 Favre**

Brett Favre now owns nine NFL career records. The statistics are through four games in 2007 and count only regular-season games.

Wins: 151
MVPs: 3
Touchdown passes: 422
Pass attempts: 8,393
Completions: 5,133
Consecutive starts (QB): 241
3,000-yard passing seasons: 15
300-plus completions in a season: 15
30-plus TD passes in a season: 8

fifth-best. Those people who've voted him those "toughest" guy awards knew what they were talking about.

So it was to no one's surprise that last winter and spring when whis-pers turned to murmurs and murmurs became newspaper and internet stories that Brett had played his last down in the NFL because his skills were diminished, the guy was coming back in 2007.

Brett Favre wasn't going to end one of the best careers in NFL his-tory on two seasons in which his effectiveness as a quarterback was hamstrung by injuries to teammates and a roster filled with players who were in grade school when he was a rookie. The Packers won only 12 times in those two years and Brett's passer ratings of 70.9 and 72.7, respectively, paled in comparison to his career mark of 85.1.

In Brett's mind, that just raised the stakes. And nobody performs better when the pot is the biggest.

So what's happened? What we've come to expect from Brett Favre: he's confounded the "experts" again, just like he did in high school and college.

The Packers are winning and Brett is chasing down receivers who've caught touchdown passes, jumping into the arms of linemen and leading cheers around Lambeau Field. Green Bay entered October leading the NFC Central at 4-0. Along the way Brett has become the NFL's career leader in victories and touchdown passes, and moved into second place on the list of consecutive starts at 241 and counting. Those first two records are the ones that catch your eye, but that third one, that sums up Brett, who already was the leader among quarterbacks. The fact the other guys in the top five are linemen says a lot.

Whenever Brett decides to leave the game he still plays with all the enthusiasm of an 8-year old in the backyard, he'll walk into the Pro Football Hall of Fame five years later. Just think. Were it not for perseverance and hard work, and the right twists of fate, one of the best quarterbacks in history may never have thrown a pass in college, let alone the NFL.

Brett Favre will be remembered in many ways. For me, none is greater than standing as a testament to beating the odds and taking his lone chance to a level even he could not have imagined.

— Coach Mark McHale

About the authors

Mark McHale has more than 30 years of football coaching experience from high school through the professional level. Recognized among the top offensive line coaches in the country, McHale has coached in eight bowl games for such schools as Southern Mississippi, Louisville, South Carolina, Marshall and Florida State. He also was a part of the coaching staff of the Frankfurt Galaxy, which won the World League of American Football championship in 1995. In addition to the WLAF, McHale also coached in the CFL. McHale, a graduate of West Virginia University, lives in Panama City Beach, Fla., with his wife Beverly. His website is www.markmchalefootball.com.

Tim Stephens, an award-winning sportswriter with "The Herald-Dispatch" in Huntington, W.Va., for more than 20 years, collaborated with Mark McHale on 10 to 4. Stephens, who is Tri-State Director of the Fellowship of Christian Athletes, has co-authored three other books, the most recent being "The Marshall Story: College Football's Greatest Comeback". He lives with his wife, Emily, in Proctorville, Ohio.

MARK McHALE

FOOTBALL

Mark McHale, the recruiter of 3 time MVP quarterback, Brett Favre, knows football. He has lived and breathed it for over 30 years. Now he is sharing his tricks of the trade with all the coaches who want to know how to play like the pros. You would have to walk many miles in his shoes before you could create a playbook like the one he has unleashed. Fortunately, you don't have to because he's already walked that line for you.

Coaches visit great coaches to receive knowledge from the best! This is your opportunity to master the game with the best offensive weaponry in the country. Currently there are two Mark McHale Playbooks for sale in our store: Pass Techniques and Run Techniques. And at this price it doesn't get any better than this!

www.markmchalefootball.com